THE WAY TO BE FREE

1992

THE
WAY
TO BE
FREE

J.G. Bennett

SAMUEL WEISER, INC.

York Beach, Maine

First published in the United States of America in1980 by
Samuel Weiser, Inc.
Box 612
York Beach, ME 03910

Reprinted, 1992

ISBN 0-87728-491-1
BJ

Cover art © Valerie Cooper, 1992
Used by kind permission.

Printed in the United States of America

The paper used in this publication meets the minimum
requirements of the American National Standard for
Permanence of Paper for Printed Library Materials
Z39.48-1984.

Contents

BEELZEBUB
REFERENCE

WHY MEN ARE NOT MEN

3RD SERIES + SCIENCE OF IDIOTISM

Book Two:
The Octave of Salvation

Foreword

This is the final volume to be published containing new material from the work of J.G. Bennett. During his life, Bennett became one of the foremost exponents of the ideas of G.I. Gurdjieff. Towards the end of his life, he gained his own freedom and spoke for himself.

This volume has two components. The first is derived from talks with some of his students in the seventies. The second comes from a piece of writing he did in the forties. The two complement each other in a striking way. We thought it better to have the practical and immediate material first and the theoretical and cosmic material second. The material is authentic and valuable to all those who are engaged seriously on the search for the Way. John Bennett's work was to help prepare for something of great significance.

Preface

The lectures which are the foundation for this book were given by J.G. Bennett at Sherborne House in the last years before his death in 1974. "Lectures" is perhaps too formal a word: they were really informal discussions with his students, which took place in a casual atmosphere once or twice a week. He had a way of penetrating to the real meaning of questions which were sometimes ineptly phrased, and often an important and power-ful idea would emerge in his reply to a halting and inarticulate attempt by a student to express a deeply–felt need or wish for enlightenment. Because the students were free to ask whatever they liked, without any formal organization, the book has a freshness and spontaneity which has not been destroyed by stylised editing. Tony Blake has made no attempt to turn the transcription into "literary language," and the discussions re-main much as they were delivered.

The school in which the discussions took place was a depart-ment of the Institute for the Comparative Study of History, Phi-losophy and the Sciences Ltd, founded by my husband in 1947. He opened the school at Sherborne House in Gloucestershire in 1971, and students came from many parts of the world to take part in ten-month courses held every year. The teaching at these courses was based on the system of G.I. Gurdjieff, who my husband regarded as his teacher, with amplifications and addi-tions of his own, derived from the personal work and experience of a long life of searching for the means of transforming and de-veloping the inner self of man.

The lectures and commentaries can be taken as a hand-book for 'beginners' who are sometimes suspicious or afraid of more abstruse works on 'spiritual' matters and it will also provide food for people with varying degrees of understanding and experience. If he had lived, the book would most certainly not have appeared in its present form, and perhaps would never have been published at all. I am grateful to Tony Blake for making it available, as I believe it deserves to be widely read.

Elizabeth Bennett
1979

Book One

The Way to Be Free

Introduction to Book One

We cannot convey the humor, the absurdity, the pathos or the wonder of those meetings in which Mr. Bennett tried again and again to share with us his vision. It was his way to work with anyone who was willing to try, which is quite the opposite to other teachers who will work only with the very few who have high capacities. He would say no-one can judge the soul of another and admit that some he had thought were beyond hope came through to something while others who had seemed in his eyes to be making progress turned out phoney. The cold reader can hardly be expected to feel the ordinary humanity of the man and his pupils from the edited versions that I have prepared and this is a real loss. There is always something humorous about people "talking about the infinite" and often the real issues had to do with the compost or the drains rather than with "other states of existence". People struggled to find a way towards a life of meaning and workable discipline beset by all the weakness that flesh is heir to.

I could say that Mr. Bennett tried to help people *to see.* The activities at Sherborne were certainly aimed at opening the inner doors of perception. But to say this is to brook misunderstanding. I am not talking about having visions with flashing lights and holy feelings. I am talking about seeing things as they are: the necessary ingredient for a purposeful life that is not an aberration or a disaster. If this awakens in us we cannot remain unchanged, because it opens a door to what is more real than "us". Ordinarily, the notion of inner perception is taken to mean that "someone" sees something. It is not like that. There does not have to be a recognisable self that sees, because seeing is primary. Our minds as they are cannot form an adequate mental image of this fact and it can only be discovered and realised through our penetration into and beyond experience.

At this time, the sense of other worlds, other dimensions, other degrees of freedom is becoming stronger in people, whether they realize it or not. This sense needs to be cultivated and guided and little that exists in contemporary Western culture is of much use. It must be protected from fantasy and strengthened through practical action.

The central theme of the book is the difference between 'work from the mind' and 'work from the essence'. Work from the mind produces skillful prisoners of illusion, but prisoners all the same. Work from the essence is the way to be free. It is centered in the heart.

The two lectures on "Outstripping Time" and "The Present Moment" were given in London during 1967. They form a link between Bennett's earlier work at Coombe Springs and what he came to later in the Sherborne experiment.

The extract on the Lord's Prayer, with which the book finishes, should be studied and meditated upon together with what Mr. Bennett has said about Gurdjieff's notion of the "cataclysm not according to law"*. There are many references to Gurdjieff in this book and we have provided little in the way of explanation of technical terms. The reader is advised to go to the sources.

A.G.E. Blake
Maryborough, Eire.
January, 1977

---

*Talks on Beelzebub's Tales, Coombe Springs Press, 1977.

Part I

Sometimes I say to myself, "There is no reason why other people should take as long a time as I have taken. I have made so many mistakes, surely I can help them not to make the same mistakes." But it is the same as with our children whom we want to save from making all the mistakes that we are now able to see. It does not work out like that. Everyone has to learn for himself, from their own experience. There are some things that are useless—and I have known it all along—for me to try to convey to you. Nothing but the bitterness of one's own experience and the joy of one's own experience can convey it.

Death

In front of death there is no place for emotion. Death is beyond that. It is necessary to live with death. It is truly not possible to be liberated from our own egoism unless we constantly live with death. But we must not live with it as if it were something to have miserable emotions about. It is not like that.

When someone we know dies, it is brought home to us. Why is it necessary to have it brought close to us when death is the surrounding condition of our kind of existence? Tens of millions of people are dying every day! It is because we have no real imagination. We have only subjective imagination. We see somebody we know lying dead before us and *this* death becomes real. When people die somewhere else, it is not real for us. The whole of mankind is caught in an inexorable position from which there is not much hope of escape. Only when we see something in front of us, when we have a shock because we see the consequences of our own stupidity, do we become aware of something. Universal stupidity or recklessness is again part of the general condition of our existence.

Yesterday we spoke about love and said that to love means to love all. It means to be able to put oneself, to feel oneself, in the place of all that exists. It is to share in the joys and sufferings of all life. But who is capable of this? Only a soul of great strength who has passed through a great deal of suffering.

We say quite glibly, "We may die at any moment." But it means nothing, if we say it or think it. Why is this? Because of man's roots, which are deeply embedded in illusion. We cannot tear ourselves out of this illusion. The illusion is so deeply built into us—to turn our backs on reality, to clutch at our dreams—that even if we are brought out of it by some shock, we go back again. Do not think that I have set myself the task of bringing you into an awareness of reality in this time that we are together. That is not possible. If some of you can do this in your life and find what it is, it will be a wonderful thing—not many people do. But at least every one of us should set ourselves not to turn our faces away.

It is very hard for me to convey this to you in a way that does not make it seem negative or unhappy. Unhappiness is really the condition of our illusory existence. It comes from there being something in us which knows that this life is not what it should be while we continue to cling to it. Everyone who lets go is happy for letting go. You oscillate between a false kind of happiness and a false kind of unhappiness. But where is there real suffering and joy? When you once begin to understand, you will no more run away from suffering than you will cling to joy; because you know that the two are twins, inseparable from each other.

Death is a reminder that everything in this world is limited and conditioned. Every opportunity is for a time. Everything is like this—given to us to make what we can of it and then *finish*. In spite of knowing about this and reminding oneself of it, to live in that way is a very big undertaking. All one's perceptions become different. Tremendous advice! But it is only empty words. Who lives this day as if it were their last? Impossible. It is impossible because we have nothing in our state to face living in that way. Side by side with illusion there is what is called in Buddhism "heedlessness," which is our enemy. We cannot heed, take note, take into ourselves the indications and signs of our lives.

With some people it is a real besetting sin to think that they know best. There is nothing in them that can resist this—at the moment they know best. It does not even occur to them to question that they know best or that what they are doing is the right thing to do. One very naturally asks, "Are these diseases of the psyche incurable?" It would be tragic if the answer were yes, because we have to live with the diseases of our own essence. There are certain things in the essence that have to be eradicated but they will not be eradicated without suffering. One person has it in the form of "he knows;" another has some kind of fear. These things are difficult to work against, and it is no use papering it all over. If I simply encourage your energies so that you can accomplish things that you could not before, and yet you remain with these underlying deficiences in your own nature, then one day it will all turn to ashes for you.

Expectation And Future Time

I want to try and explain why expectations can prevent things from happening.

The real reason is that we live in different worlds and in these worlds different kinds of things can happen. One way of talking about it is to say that the different worlds are on different levels and correspond to different levels of consciousness. The evidence that we do live in such different worlds is not hard to find. For example, there are about forty people here taking part in what seems to be one event. In reality, some are in one world and others are in other worlds, on different levels. Afterward, if you compare notes, you will find that some of you heard or perceived quite different things than others. But it is not simply a matter of selective hearing and subjective bias: the actual events in the different worlds are different.

This is because the nature of events in the different worlds is not the same. There is a mechanical world in which events are governed by some kind of cause and effect. All of the events in this world are of the same kind and cannot be any different. They make up the world that science studies: a quantitative world in which the future can be predicted. This means, for example. that it is possible to design an atomic bomb on paper simply through calculation. If such events were the only events—if there were only the mechanical world—there would be nothing to be done. But the world of our mental experience is different from that. It has much more freedom and elasticity in it so it is essentially not predictable. Even our experience of the material world contains much that is not predictable. We come under many different lines of causality and the interplay is uncertain.

Consider the case of an accident. For this to occur a car has to be coming in this direction and another in that direction and the state of mind of the people involved has to be such and such. All of these are quite independent and it is only when there is a certain combination of material objects and states of mind of people that an accident occurs. For this reason, though you may say that this person will have an accident sooner or later, you cannot predict when or what kind of accident it will be. Although every part of it is governed by causal laws, as far as the people involved are concerned, it is still unpredictable because of the uncertainty of the manner in which the different lines will come in contact with each other.

Beyond this, there are worlds where we ourselves are able to influence the course of events: where our will, our understanding, and our judgement come into play. These are the worlds in which we are interested.

Before we can hope to understand these higher worlds, we must understand that the material world is completely closed to change. It is the world *surface.* We live in it for most of the time.* It is not only predictable by calculation: it is possible to be in contact with it in a direct way. It was an experience of this kind that awakened my interest in these matters. While I was living in Turkey in 1919, I had a very vivid dream: I was standing with my back to a wall watching a fire. I saw a great crowd of people, and furniture was being thrown out of a window to be caught by the firemen. Then, some kind of wardrobe came out of the window and the firemen, who obviously thought they could not catch it, got out of the way. It crashed on the ground and I saw it collapse. Five days after the dream occurred, I heard the shout of a fire warning. By then I had quite forgotten about the dream and went out of curiosity to see where the fire was. I found myself standing just as I had in my dream and saw the same things happen. But the moment I remember most was when I began to think, "Now, will that wardrobe come out of the window or not?" It made an extraordinary impression on me when it actually came out and I saw it crash.

I said to myself; "All our understanding about time is wrong. In some way the future exists, or I couldn't have seen that fire five

---

*The nature of the different worlds we live in is extensively discussed in Bennett's *Deeper Man*, Turnstone Press, 1978.

days before it happened." This led me to study premonitory phemomena. Later, I had various kinds of experience, but none so bright and sharp as that. I read Mire's book, *Les Pheno-menon Premonitoire,* a study of all the premonitions of the First World War that he collected. Many people saw someone close to them being killed, or saw such things as walls falling down under bombardment, things which they did not understand at the time. He was able to reconstruct a number of these and show that they were connected with actual events. But he noticed that no one had predicted the outcome of the war and nobody had any premonitions of states of mind or decisions: all the premonitions concerned material events. It was this that first put me on the track of different worlds, including worlds beyond prediction.

The events that really matter to us are the ones belonging to the higher worlds. These events are not mechanical and do not belong to the predictable future. That is where we make difficulties for ourselves by having expectations. If we are looking toward something joyful, we should realise that this is something that belongs to a higher world. It is not a mechanical thing. We should not treat it as we would a material event. On the other hand, the state of foreboding we can get into, when we feel that something dreadful is about to happen, must inevitably be in relation to some material event, such as having an accident, losing our money, and so on. When we have a state of identification, which is in this case both expectation and foreboding, we bring ourselves down into the mechanical world. We get caught in that world and, to all intents and purposes, are just a walking "thing." We bring ourselves into the way of "things."

If something is to happen that may be of interest and significance, our excessive identification with the thought of it can so bring us down that we run the risk of by-passing the event altogether—*because we are in the wrong world.* If we get into a state of foreboding, of anxiety and worry, we bring ourselves down and run headlong into the very thing we are worrying about. We would by-pass what we are anxious about if only we did not worry—because then we would be in a different world. The irony is that identification with the future runs one into the risk of missing the good things and going headlong into the bad ones. That is why so many distressful things happen to people who are always worrying. We tend to say, "Well, they bring their own troubles on themselves." They do not bring their troubles on themselves; they bring themselves into the world where troubles occur. There are people with excessive expectations, who are always thinking and talking about the good things that are going to happen. How often the things they expect fail to happen!

In the very same way we can become identified with the past—brood over injuries and failures and so on—and this again means that we bring ourselves down. This is the essence of identification. When one is identified, one makes oneself like a mechanical object and all the corresponding mechanical events happen to us. This is why non-identification, detachment, and inner freedom are so important if one wants to find a really satisfying life. The really satisfying world—the world of feeling, of exciting and worthwhile events—is there all the while as long as one is not oneself a "thing." If one lets oneself become a "thing," one simply lives in a mechanically predictable world. There are people whose lives become pathetically predictable. You know what they will be doing in a year, in five years, to the end of their lives. They will be playing bridge as long as they can hold the cards in their hands.

This leads me to talk about a certain kind of work. Two or three times I have read to you Gurdjieff's lecture on *Freedom and Pride,** and in that lecture he speaks about how we must struggle with identification. We have to do it by reasoning with ourselves.

This is a kind of work that has to be done entirely in the mind. It has to be done immediately when there is the need. It is possible for us to work on our mental states and attitudes. We have the power, at least for a time, to change them. So that if I see myself expecting something, I then say that I will not; instead, I shall think of something different. Of course, in practice the change only lasts for a few moments and the original state returns. But at least we know that for that time, which may be seconds, may be minutes, we can turn our attention from one mental occupation to another.

---

*cf., "Liberation leads to liberation," *Views from the Real World,* G.I. Gurdjieff, Routledge & Kegan Paul, 1975. This contains an edited version.

There is something that is more permanent. We can change our whole attitude toward expectations. Instead of regarding them as something harmless we begin to see and understand that their effect is always negative. Identification with the future diminishes our chances and closes down our potential; it brings us into a lower level world. It was not until I had understood all this for myself and became quite convinced of it that I found I was able to get rid of expectations and stop worrying about the future.

This is not to say that one should never calculate. Where it is possible to calculate, one should do so. If I am going to cook a meal I must know that I am going to have the ingredients there tomorrow and how much I am going to use. That is because such things belong to that kind of world. I know the things I can do by day and I know the things I can do by night.

The technique of reasoning with yourself is something you do entirely in your mind. You have to get yourself into your mind and see the absurdity of what is going on. That is all. Gurdjieff called this work *active mentation*. It takes you out of the passive state of expecting and fearing. When something can be done in the mind and can only be done in the mind, then that is where it has to be done. It is a matter of putting one's understanding against one's mechanical habits. It is not of any use to do breathing exercises, sensing or the like, except to put yourself into a good state: the actual exercise itself goes on entirely in the mind. There has to be an understanding before we can act as the affirming force in this kind of exercise. When we come to have a *conviction* that these apparently harmless mental processes to do with expectation are in fact depriving us of possibilities, we can make an affirmation. Something in us can then say, "This is to stop," and it will.

What I am saying is really not easy to grasp—it is so contrary to our usual ways of thinking. It is so firmly fixed in us that there is only one world—the world of material changes—that we go on all the time thinking and acting as if it were really so. Even then we do not experience life as if it were like that. For example, we have all sorts of emotional states which would be totally meaningless if only the mechanical world existed. So in our emotions, we are living as if there were more than one world, while in our thinking we are living as if there is only one. Our feelings are much more free than our minds, but the trouble is that the problem of expectation has to be solved in our thinking.

A lot of events are necessary ones. We have to live with our bodies. It's important to be able to recognise when we are going out of the realm of "cause and effect," where calculation is applicable, into realms where it is not. Nearly all of what are called psychic phenomena are simply events belonging to a not very high but different world which has some freedom in it. That is why all the scientific attempts to make sense of psychic phenomena are absurd, for what distinguishes these phenomena is that they do not have the predictability of the material world.

It is also absurd to treat our communication with each other as something predictable. This is strikingly obvious in the realm of the highly organised communication media. The media people believe that they control the opinion of the world. They think that it is *they* who have access to the good stories and unless they put something across it will not get known. In fact, a great deal gets known by word-of-mouth. People are interested in what other people have done and what others have found. This means more to them than any kind of impersonal presentation, no matter how sophisticated.

More people become interested in this Work through other people than by any other means. Most of the people you can speak to—or at least half—will be interested rather than not. Therefore the question of whether we should take the initiative in speaking, or whether we should wait until asked is an important one. Gurdjieff was very insistent that we should speak about the Work "in season and out of season"—the words that St. Paul used when talking about preaching the Gospel. People laughed at this and Gurdjieff did not like it when they laughed. I believe that he meant it seriously: people should carry Beelzebub* around with them, read it on the train, in cafes, waiting rooms and so on.

The way in which people come together round these ideas is very interesting. There is probably some kind of unorganized brotherhood built on a certain affinity. It is not possible to make a rule about what we should do about it. When I first came into

*Gurdjieff's book *Beelzebub's Tales to His Grandson*, Routledge & Kegan Paul, 1977.

contact with this Work and we were trying to get people to-gether, I was one of the ones who would chat to people any-where and at any time and bring them along to lectures and meetings. It was one's role at that stage. But there are dangers of spoiling the Work for others. For example, if one tries to bring children to it, it is very noticeable. They may have a psychokin-etic nature, but at the same time they will be suspicious on the personality level. I remember how it was for Lonya, Madame Ouspensky's grandson. He had a very strong desire for the Work, but all the time scoffed at the people involved, saying, "These idiots who run after my grandfather or my grand-mother. . . they just don't understand anything; they are just idiots." All attempts to interest him in the Work just put him off more and more and things came to a tragic end (though with his sister it was quite different).

You have to remember not to urge children to read books about the Work, or to urge them to take part in some Work activity. We have, as you know, some teenage girls here and sometimes I wonder whether it is right to offer them nothing connected with the Work, because all they do is sit in their rooms and play re-cords. But I am sure that this is the right way. Any attempts to bring them into the Work will spoil it for them later on.

It goes back to Moses: one is taken and the other left. This always seems sad—but what does it mean? It means that if you have a psychokinetic nature, then you also have a responsibil-ity to the question that was put in front of you when you were given this particular nature. It was not just for yourself, but for a high purpose, because such relatively liberated beings are nec-essary. It is not permitted that you should allow yourself the usual sort of life. What is perfectly legitimate and harmless in psycho-static people cannot be allowed in people who have the possibility of transformation. It is extremely awkward.

Say to one's parents and family what they want to hear. This is "external considering" and it is the right thing to do. It is not in-sincere. To tell people things that they do not want to hear is in-terfering with their lives, which is worse than insincerity.

When people become involved in the Work they do not know what is happening to them nor why it is happening. I can cer-tainly say for myself that I got caught in this Work without knowing what had happened to me. Afterwards I saw that I was really caught. I cannot say that it was my choice. The *magnetic center** is deeper than the mind. It is something centered in our will, in the very core of our being; but in order to become operative it has to have some contact with the outside world. This contact has to come through the personality and so there is an hazardous situation. A person can have a psychokinetic nature and have no means of responding to it, because there is no food coming from the environment or the environment is unfavorable. And the converse can happen: the environment is favorable when the inner possibility is not there and a pseudo-magnetic center forms, which sooner or later shows its insubstantiality.

We used to believe that there were only a few people who have a psychokinetic nature and that this Work was for the few. This was certainly the way we looked at it fifty-odd years ago. Either we were wrong or times have changed, because at this time there is a very high proportion of people who, if it is presented to them in a way that they can recognise, will respond to the psychokinetic idea. I think that half the mistake was in restricting it to a particular pattern. The Work was taken in too narrow a way. I think that more people with a psychokinetic nature are being born now than were a hundred or fifty years ago. This has happened because these people are needed.

I spoke about the ineffectiveness of the media. The truth is that the media are geared to one world. Even when they take upon themselves to talk about other worlds, they always return to the mechanical one. Even the second world—the world of the psyche, if you like, though it is more than that—cannot be spoken about in this popular manner and produce an effective communication. Of course, people who are searching can follow very slender clues; but, generally speaking, all that is abroad in the media relates to one world and people have become so accustomed to it that it is almost impossible to think in any other way. If, somehow, people feel the need for some other world, then they must think of another world as coming after death; or as accessible for a very few people of exceptional being needing special conditions of life. This is all a mistake.

---

*Term used by Gurdjieff to speak about spontaneous attraction to the Work. *cf.,* *In Search of the Miraculous,* P.D. Ouspensky, Routledge & Kegan Paul, 1950, p.200-204.

The worlds interpenetrate one another: they are compresent; they are in the same place. Here we are, sitting together in this room at this moment, yet we are in different worlds. Some are aware of it; others are not. It is extremely hard to take it literally. Psychologically, it is pretty easy: some people understand what is being said, others find that it passes over their heads or does not even exist for them. But what is really going on is not only connected with one's inner state. The objective difference shows itself in the way in which people are connected. In the first, (material) world, they are connected from the outside; for example, through the media of sight and sound. In the second, they meet each other differently and there is no need for the external communication. In still higher worlds the connection between people is different again and therefore different things happen to them. The relationship between the sexes is different in the three different worlds.

Here in this place we can sometimes be aware of sharing more than one world. It is very important and it is enduring and will not be lost. But when we go away from here and from the conditions here, we will go to where it is assumed that there is only one world. Whatever people may think, however they may talk about mind, and spirit, and feelings, and so on, what they are really talking about the whole time is one world in which everything is outside of everything else.

Even in order to breathe properly, we have to be in more than one world. Breathing is different in each of the worlds. The significance of the *zikr* is an action that belongs to the second world. The significance of food and its possibilities of transformation is that man should be able to live in more than one world. The last words of the last book that Gurdjieff wrote say that it is possible for man to live equally in three worlds.

I must tell you that I have never found a way of getting this across to people unless they have experienced it for themselves. It remains only words. It is not something that can be conveyed to another person by words. I deferred talking about it until now at the very end of the Course, after we have been through so many experiences together that unmistakeably point to different worlds. But I know how easy it is for everything that I have said to turn into something ordinary. The reason for this is that the apparatus which we call the *centers* in us—the way we think, the way we feel and so on—is really only for this world. There are other instruments for perceiving and living in the higher worlds. So we are asking impossible things of our minds. What we have to do is to free ourselves from expectation and all the blind habits of thought that bring us down. If something has awakened for you about all this, then it is a most precious possession and you must do everything you can to substantiate it. It is an unlimited way.

Personality

(A reply to observations by someone who had decided not to smoke.)

You saw that smoking a cigarette had a specific effect on your ability to sense yourself or to bring about some movement of energies in yourself. You accidentally saw this and spoke to me about it and I was able to recognise that you had found yourself in a place where you have a different kind of freedom. There you were free from yourself and could take decisions.

People live their lives on a level of themselves where there is hardly any freedom or capacity to determine what will happen. That is personality. As I said to one of the groups earlier today, it is a very hard thing to accept that the personality is really helpless and empty. It has no more capacity for independent initiative than a suit of clothes. A suit of clothes will move about and change its shape if it has a body inside it that will move about, but ordinarily it is inert. It is the same with personality. It will move about so long as there are various urges arising in us and as long as there are situations coming from outside. You can see this time and time again and still not be convinced about it. For example, in the *stop exercise* you may see many times that at that moment there is nobody there and you can even say to yourself, "Well, now I can really see that there is no 'I' in my personality; it is just an automaton," but it still doesn't come home to you. You can see it a hundred times and it does not come home. One reason is that it is terrifying. "If I am empty, if there is no one there, what is to become of me?" So we shut it off and the realization does not become part of us.

My task, if it is possible in the time, is to help those who so wish to understand the reality of this sort of thing.

In 1923, Gurdjieff gave a lecture about this theme. Unfortunately, most of it was lost, but I retained some notes and I remember the strange diagram that he drew of the different centers and the formatory apparatus. He said something like this, "You are taught that you are three-centered beings, that you have thinking center, emotional center, moving center and this is how you live. But in reality man does not live like this—man lives with only one thing and that is with his formatory apparatus, because that is all his personality can live with." Then he drew the diagram in which there was a little piece of mechanism in the front rather like a fan with an axle behind it. It was simply blowing out whatever came from behind it; puffing it out into the open. He drew arrows showing that the intellectual center had no means of expression through the personality. The personality can only express itself through the ready-made words, ideas, habitual expressions, and so on, that are stored up in the formatory apparatus. Nothing comes directly from the centers, nothing goes directly to the centers. Man does not live even in the lower part of himself. He lives in an artificial shell that surrounds it.

The problem is to be able to see this for oneself and understand that it is so, acquiring a permanent change of attitude towards one's own personality. It is not capable of developing. It has no potential for transformation into anything. Everything worthwhile depends on our liberation from personality and our coming into essence, so that essence has the initiative.

Accidentally, we can make a shift. R talked about seeing smoking from a different part of himself. He was seeing it from his essence. He could see that it was largely something in his personality. It was the same with D, who made a momentary shift that had nothing to do with efforts or merits. She also became aware that there was a possiblity of deciding to stop smoking. Something like this has to be reinforced by the decision exercise, because, as she was describing to us, the personality will start inventing reasons for smoking again. This is partly connected with the personality not wanting to give up the position it has occupied in us until now.

Gurdjieff talks about the fictitious consciousness, that man calls his consciousness, and the *real* consciousness. It all refers to this. It is not something impossibly remote. If you really wish to be free from this state of illusion, it is possible for you. But you must never spoil your vision. If you see something, never start explaining it or trying to do something with it. The moment of vision is sufficient and efficacious in itself.

The personality will channel everything through the formatory apparatus. Again and again people have essence perceptions, but always their personality intercepts them when they come into their consciousness and turns them into words, emotions, or anything except the simple direct awareness. This messing about with what we see is a tremendous thief of opportunity.

I remember when I first really saw these things. It was in 1933 when I was going down to a Summer school with Ouspensky. Ouspensky said that we would stop the night in Gadsden, Kent, and go down to Shoreham in the morning. He liked to talk interminably about things and, if one had the stamina for it, one could sit all night through until daybreak or later with him drinking bottle after bottle of claret, which was a weakness of his. So we sat talking all night and then in the morning I drove down to the coast. At one moment the whole thing became clear to me. I saw how I was living my life in an unreal way, that everything was just words and I had no contact with reality at all. I saw that there was nothing I could expect; that nothing could happen to my personality. It didn't matter whether it was good or bad, clever or stupid, it had no potential. The journey took two hours and I was not really in a fit state to drive a car. But for the whole way I was in a state of complete clarity. I remember thinking to myself that it was just ten years since I had first heard these ideas and I had thought that I had really grasped what they were about; but until that minute I had no real understanding of the difference between "personality" and "essence."

Moral Discipline

One must set oneself radically to change the balance between the negative or destructive influences and the positive or creative ones. This does not mean that one must destroy the negativity in oneself. The Shivapuri Baba* sometimes expresses it in this way, but to my mind it is a misunderstanding. It is in man's nature to have negative impulses, not simply in his upbringing or through faulty heredity. But the balance between the positive and the negative is not good and dealing with negativity is grossly misunderstood in the modern world because moral discipline is looked upon as something external. The application of external morality produces all sorts of absurdities and contradictions, because what has been handed down does not correspond to the conditions of modern life. People try to look for other criteria. This can only be our conscience; but for our conscience to work we must open the way to it. It has been clearly established that people do not find the way to their own conscience unless they establish a separation between the affirming and denying parts of themselves.

We are not after making life into something grim and hard. People I know who live in this way are very happy people indeed. I must say that every time I have disciplined myself—and I am not trying to pretend that I am a well-disciplined person—I have always had greater rejoicing and satisfaction and feelings of

---

*cf., J.G. Bennett, *Long Pilgrimage*, Turnstone Press 1975. The Shivapuri Baba was a Nepalese saint who died in 1963. He taught the three disciplines: physical, moral, spiritual. Physical discipline is duty, skill and right living. Moral discipline is purification of mind. Spiritual discipline is meditation and God realisation.

freedom and well-being. Making discipline into something grim and hard is entirely a matter of our own egoism: we turn it into a virtue and begin to think of ourselves as "better." It seems that whenever we do something good our self-love swallows it up. But this will not happen if we keep ourselves in a state of rejoicing, because rejoicing and self-love are not compatible with each other.

However, if we wish to establish a really effectual communication between the inner and the outer parts of our nature. then we must clear away the obstacles which are in the lower nature. But when you know how to use the energies that are released by self-denial you will find it much less painful than you expected.

Inner Considering

S: I had something to say at a meeting and I could not bring myself to speak. I noticed that the energy I had to say this thing turned into myself: I became "justification" and "inner considering." So I see that what has been happening to me is just that I've been persisting in my pattern of not being able to be vulnerable in front of people.

JGB: But I know that you have also had the experience of breaking out of this imaginary prison in which you shut yourself up. It is very much due to your imagination, connected with the feeling that you won't be accepted, that you won't be understood, that if you try something it won't come off properly and you will fail. If you have experienced the taste of being able to get out of this negative imagination, you must also see that you do not lose it. So it is a good thing that you got yourself to speak this evening.

What is inner considering? One aspect is making demands—even if they are hidden demands that do not show on the outside—on other people. Instead of being concerned with understanding other people, we are concerned with whether they will understand us. We even *demand* that they should understand us and make life easier for us by understanding our difficulties. This is a real obstacle and prevents us from reaching our own essence. The reason for it is real but it is misinterpreted. You have a lack of confidence; you do not know how people will respond, or you fear that they will not respond in an encouraging way to anything that you might say or do. At the bottom of it all there is something that knows that you are out of contact with your own self. This produces a feeling of helplessness, sometimes even of despair. Just where there ought to be something in us that is confident and self-reliant, able to bear things, something is missing because of the separation between the personality and the "I" , or fundamentally, between the "I" and the center which are working without their Master. For everyone, this produces a latent feeling of insecurity. Everyone is insecure until they know that the "I" and their center are connected with one another. We want to know that there is someone in us who can take decisions, is not afraid of taking them and facing their consequences. When there is that, this kind of suffering gives way.

Part II

If I look back, I have to say that without Gurdjieff I would be very small indeed and it was largely through having the benefit of his most extraordinary search and sacrifice that I and others have had possibilities.

Not everything came from him, but the possiblity of making use of what I found, I owe very much to him. This isn't to say that he didn't make mistakes, or that he found the best way of helping people in this day and age. But he was a pioneer of extraordinary courage—daring one might say—he tried things that people had not tried before and under different conditions of life than we have here.

Thanks to his having been willing to expose himself to extreme dangers and a kind of suffering that is not easy to understand, things were opened for us. But it is totally foolish to think of him as infallible. Even the perfected man is not free from mistakes. <u>The further one goes, the more pitfalls. . .</u>

MANY PITFALLS, FOR ANYONE WHO THINKS AND ACTS AS AN INDIVIDUAL—
AN `I' ? —

Pattern

Sometimes in reading *Beelzebub's Tales* to you I have shown that there is a pattern beneath the surface. Sometimes some of you have seen it for yourselves. One of the purposes of our kind of work is to develop the power to discern the hidden pattern in things. You will remember Gurdjieff describing how it is possible by knowing one part of the human body to know all the rest. That is what it is like to see the pattern.

One way of expressing this idea is to say that there is hidden order behind the apparent disorder, or a hidden purpose behind the visible absence of purpose. Part of our task of becoming conscious beings, able to act intentionally, is to bring the hidden pattern into the visible world. In the chapter, *Purgatory*, Gurdjieff refers to this. He says that Our Endlessness foresaw the possibility, through three-brained-beings, of finding a help for himself in the "administration of the enlarging world." This conveys the sense of man being a link between the visible and the invisible worlds, not only in perceiving the invisible and entering with his consciousness into the world of values but also of bringing into the visible world a work of realising the pattern and purpose of things.

We labor under the misapprehension that we have to think up what we have to do. The truth is that this is not our responsibility, because the pattern of things is far greater than we can imagine.

In the building of the great cathedrals of the Middle Ages, the whole plan was in the mind of the architect, but the detailed working out was left to the craftsmen who had freedom of expression. If their work was not in harmony with the whole, it was thrown out. The craftsmen had to be sensitive to the plan. People were prepared over a very long time to be able to teach the craftsmen to have that kind of perception.

You must always remember the principle of beginning with what is commensurate with your powers. Gurdjieff always said that people try to do what is too big for them and they neglect to do what is within their power. In the chapter on *War* he ascribes the reiterated failure of the organizations to stop war to their attempting something which is quite outside of man's power at this stage. People neglect the things that it would be possible for them to do. Gurdjieff emphasised the importance of communication and said that what was required was that there should be one language, one religion, one center of advice and counselling. With moderate success in this direction they were able to move toward getting rid of the terrible situation that existed in the twelfth, thirteenth and fourteenth centuries in central Asia.

We, because we are three-brained-beings, have a capacity for creating order. Certainly insects produce miracles of orderly patterning, but it is not their own intentional and conscious action. It is the creative action of some extraordinary intelligence that, for some reason not easy to understand, brought these prodigious powers of the insects into the visible world. Some people think that it was an experiment in preparation for three-brained-beings. Others think that the insects themselves were originally three-brained-beings who in some way betrayed the task which they were brought to do and were therefore deprived of the power of intentional action. Whatever happened, the insect world is an amazing experience. We can have this power intentionally. What are we doing about it? Ibsen's *Peer Gynt* has always served me as a warning.

Bring it down to your immediate perceptions. You are constantly handling material objects of all kinds. What is the pattern that can come in? When you are cooking, be sensitive to that pattern. If everything goes as it should, than that pattern will have been realized. This will not be a small thing, because something will have entered into reality by that. You should learn to notice when you lose contact with the pattern. The loss of contact will be due to your carelessness or self-will.

You are working at doing a specific task each day. You should create the pattern very clearly in your mind and bring it into a mental vision. There is one spontaneous moment when what you will do occurs to you; "*That's* what I'll do." You have to learn how to come to that without forcing it. Maybe some of you have observed the difference between something that comes to us in that form and something we have to search for and put together by thinking it all out. It is the same with the role-playing exercises you have been doing. I say that the same process is required there: there should be a spontaneous arising of a pattern in one's mind which one then clothes in the form of action with people and characteristics and then it has life and will play itself.

Do a thing rightly and you will not have the necessity of making yourself do it rightly the next time. If you do not interfere, it will do itself again. We have the power in us to create a thought form or pattern. It can come by repetition or be entirely created in our inner vision. The important case is when we create an image and project it into the future. The ability to be connected with the future is something that we have to work at. Many of you have found that when you project an image into the future, it seems that the material situation adapts itself to you and things work out by themselves. It is not really that things have adapted to you, but that something in you has made a connection with what is really possible at a given moment in the future.

Some people have that capacity developed in them and they have surprising achievements. Usually, they end by spoiling it. They start to think they are doing something and making something happen, whereas, they are really in a kind of clairvoyant connection with the pattern of the future. Anyone who has studied Napoleon's campaigns will know how he was able to see what would happen in a battle and how he would wait for that moment and take advantage of it when it did happen. Then he lost his capacity and everything went wrong for him. His own picture of himself took the place of this simple perceptiveness. This has happened with more than one successful person. It very seldom happens that people who acquire this power accidentally are able to keep the right attitude towards it. They don't recognize that it is not their own doing and has nothing to do with their being or quality. For the man who is looked upon as someone who can achieve what he sets out to do, it is extraordinarily hard to maintain the awareness that he simply has the capacity to read the course of events and adapt himself to them, not to influence them.

Another State of Existence

S: I was working at the . . . exercise and came to the image of Christ. Things seemed to disappear and were more refined. I felt that freedom would be something where there are no material things—something transparent, where I would not be identified. I had this strong taste and then I looked at it and said, "My God, what really is this feeling?" I could not identify anything. I could not say that I was aware. I could say I was observing myself, but what was in this freedom was not there anymore, there was nothing. Later on I wondered if it was just an association with a thought form. I have had it several times since.

JGB: The same taste of freedom?

S: Yes. It has made me much aware of what is inner and outer. I thought I knew about that before, but the taste is very different now. But I do not know what the inner is in any descriptive terms.

JGB: What we are concerned with now is being able to take ourselves out of an illusory world into a world which, although it is still quite limited and conditioned, is a world of real experiencing. This is the main thing we are concerned with. Now this is not all—there are worlds that are entirely different which cannot be grasped by the human mind. It is not impossible for us accidentally to come under some influence coming from such a world, and when we do there is (for the time being) a transformation in our state. In your example, it came partly because you put your attention on Christ as representing a very high quality of being; it can also happen that people feel a different state of existence and have no idea how it came about.

S: I had two experiences this week. In the first I was unhappy for a day or two; but not unhappy about being unhappy. This was a real difference. I felt so much more in touch with myself. I tried to write about my unhappiness and I got the feeling that somehow I was much closer to my own nothingness. The thing that came to me, almost in a sense of despair, was the difference between feeling I was empty and seeing that I was really "nothing." I felt genuine in some way. There was still some fear to do with that. Though I was "nothing," there was still so much I needed, and could "nothing," get something?

In the second experience I had the same sense of helplessness, but it was outward going rather than inward going. I saw that all of us were, and are, helpless. I strongly wished I could be like that always.

JGB: It has a little of the quality of homesickness. Homesickness is a reflection of this thing in us, which is an experience brought about by something outside of ourselves. The technical name for this in Sufism is *jazba* and in Greek it is *sterisis* or privation. It is a spiritual homesickness. It is necessary for us. Sometimes it remains in our heart most of the time. There are periods one goes through when one is constantly aware of a sense of being bereft of something. It is also possible, as you say, to have this not only on one's own behalf.

When this feeling comes we have to watch over our purity and not misuse it. The feeling is itself authentic and is an indication of being near to something. One doesn't really feel deprived until one is close.

We are brought close to it again and again and something prevents us from going the last step. Either we spoil it for ourselves by thinking about it, or there is some inability in us which spoils it for us. Maybe it's simply that we are not yet strong enough to take the next step.

Sometimes we have the feeling, "If I had not panicked, something would have happened to me." What makes us panic is the inability to accept our own nothingness: it looks as if there is a darkness ahead of us and we are frightened of going into that darkness. It is not at all something to be afraid of, but it is impossible to know what it is until one goes through it.

Efforts

JGB: In the first stage of relaxation one can sense the muscles relaxing and one's body coming into a more stable and balanced posture. When it comes to the deeper relaxing, there is nothing that can be perceived in this way and therefore it is very difficult to verify.

The connection between efforts and the changes that are consequent on efforts is often surprising. We do not easily see the underlying patterns and connections or the network of influences that are working.

S: Many times, I've seen the connection between cleaning something with my body—my room for example—and finding that my inside, my mind, is more in order.

JGB: A good observation. It is a matter of a vertical connectiveness between one level of ourselves and another that one cannot understand in terms of cause and effect.

S: At the evening meal I was watching the waiters serving and the people eating, and I was in contact with what was around me. The things that were going on seemed to be unique and although I've seen somebody serving tables a thousand times before, I was noticing qualities that will never be repeated again.

JGB: Your description refers to what I talked about before, a shift in yourself from one place to another. You look at the same event, but from a different perspective. In most cases you don't look at it at all, you are just mechanically inserted into the cogwheels of the events that are going on. You talk and observe and study and consider that you are three-centered-beings because you observe a difference between thinking and feeling and so on. What you don't see is that the whole of this has been put through a mincing machine. It all becomes the same sort of thing when it goes through the formatory apparatus. It is comparatively rare that we have direct center perceptions and then they always have this freshness and directness that you describe, when everything is interesting. For the personality it is not like that.

This doesn't mean that our personality has to be destroyed or put out of action. But our whole attitude towards it has to change. The shift of perspective has to be made permanent. One thing that can help us a lot is to see the complete mechanicalness of our associations. The trouble is that we accept that only sometimes. We think that sometimes we are asleep and sometimes not. It is very difficult to accept that the very nature of our personality is to be an automaton. That is why it comes under all kinds of influences that are unnatural and absurd for it to come under. Its opinions, attitudes, interests, and so on, can be changed without its even noticing.

What matters for us in our time here is to look at ourselves from all sides—when we are doing movements, doing the morning exercise, or when we have this spontaneous waking up. The frequency of the spontaneous moments is greatly increased by the efforts we are making. The reward of making efforts is not, in general, to bring about change; it is to create possibilities for us, to open the way to our having spontaneous experiences. But the trouble is that we can make the efforts, we can have the spontaneous perceptions and, at the very moment when something good is coming into our hands, we throw it away by letting our personality steal it.

JGB: For many years I used to wait at meals when we went to the Ouspensky's for weekends. It is astonishing how useful these simple things are. You can feel the difference between the pattern, the right way of doing it, and what you, neglecting and shirking, are making of it. It produces in us a state of self-observation.

S: I made a decision that was beyond my power to accomplish. To correct that I thought I would give up a meal, because I thought that that would be hard for me. I anticipated an extremely difficult struggle but as yesterday came round, breakfast passed and then I missed lunch and dinner. There was no struggle, it seemed very right and just that I did miss these meals.

JGB: Do you remember in *Beelzebub's Tales* Hassein asking what is objective right and wrong? Beelzebub had been talking about the absurdiy of our ideas of good and evil as things external to ourselves. He said "right is that from which our conscience can be at rest and peace." *YEAH, MAN! HOO HA! QM*

The completing of a cycle puts one at peace. The decision has to be fulfilled in some way. It is so constructed that we can have this second opportunity. If the decision was made and there was some mistake in the way we made the decision, then it carries on to the next stage and we have to bring our bodies into it directly. We talk about "punishing ourselves" but that is a very poor way of putting it. It misses the real point about the action which comes here. There is something about it that is quite unmistakeable—a real quality, the quality of sacrifice.

You sacrificed your comfort and desire for food so that your body will be brought into the work in a way that it hadn't been before. It is a great objective. We should be reborn or have the birth of the real man in us. Those who have passed through this process have really died. It is through conscience that we can come to the moment of *the day of judgement* in ourselves. God comes so close to man through his conscience that this is able to be something direct for each one of us.

Two Principles of Living

JGB: I want to remind you of Beelzebub's distinction between the two principles of living—the *foolasnitamnian* and the *itoklanoz*. I have yet to find out how he derived these words, but he always used them. *Foolasnitamnian* is the right way for a three-brained-being to be living. When a man is able to live that, he is able to fulfill his destiny and he will not leave this world until he has completed the formation of his *kesdjan* body. We are talking about something which is the aim of our lives. The other way is where one lives by external shocks, particularly by the causes that have arisen in the past. In the way of *itoklanoz* we are living in the action of our past lives: the *bobbin-kandlenosts*, the wound up springs that keep us moving, simply go on until they are exhausted and then leave nothing behind. Living as a result of causes depends on whether the causes were produced intentionally or not. If not, then there is what Gurdjieff called "living under the law of accident." It is one of the first things from which a man can become free. The essential thing is to put oneself under the laws of the work or under the laws of some definite purpose to be fulfilled. It is the act of commitment, which by itself changes our relationship to the law of accident.

The *itoklanoz* way of living is that of a marionette with a lot of threads attached to different parts, each of which are producing reactions and behaviour manifestations. With the *foolasnitamnian* there is something that is holding it together and it is woven according to a purpose that goes beyond the present. For each one of us there is a pattern of life which is our destiny. In the realization of this we fulfill the reason for our existence here on earth. There is also the pattern of the day and the pattern of the hour. To see this requires a certain kind of awareness. The direct perception of our pattern belongs to conscience and the unconditioned side of our nature. The pattern is creative and created.

The confidence has to grow in us all that each of us has a pattern in our lives, each of us has a destiny, and all will go as it should if we can get close enough to it—to be fully in is very much to hope for. For some of you, your lives were going against your true pattern before you came here. The feeling of tension this brought about was one of the factors that brought you here. You have felt the need to be able to do what is right for you. This is something that we can gradually work at and not just think and talk about. It can be brought into everything that we do whether it is something outward, like the cooking of a meal, or something inward like the morning exercise. We are trying to get this pattern of the wholeness of our lives into our awareness.

If it were not for the pattern of events in human history, then man's disorganising power would destroy the whole of life. Rare people can produce extraordinary events in the world because they are endowed with pattern awareness. By taking things within the scale of our own lives we can have a taste of this very special thing. Then our lives are not just the working out of the consequences of past causes, but have a creative feeling in them.

S: I was able to compose music that fitted for the play. I don't know how it came about; it was one of those things that were there already. I wasn't even conscious at all of; "Oh my God, it is coming to me." It was sort of there. I think it was like an acceptance of some sort, but required a certain amount of opening. You can participate in something, but as long as you have preconceived ideas of what you are, it seems to leave you out. You have to accept yourself to fit into some kind of pattern.

JGB: Right. I must say that I did notice the music and I was quite sure that it had been composed as you described. You never get things like that if you think them out. However much trouble you take, there is always something that doesn't fit. There is a big element of trust in this. You see that there is something that you can trust, and if you trust it will go on and keep things right. <u>One can do extraordinary things with the help of trust but if the trust wavers, one falls in.</u>

I talked to some people—George and Helen Sandwith—who studied the fire walkers in Fiji and elsewhere. The fire walkers said that you simply had to trust yourself to the fire. You can see that it is like that—if you trust the fire then it will not burn you. I have seen the same thing with dervishes doing all sorts of incredible things like sticking skewers through themselves and slicing themselves up with knives. They would just wipe their hands over the wounds and you would see a great big gash healing up in front of your eyes. They talk of putting their trust in God. But what are they trusting in doing that? They are not trusting God to put his hand out of heaven and haul them off the fire. They are really trusting in the pattern of the event. But you can lose your nerve and the contact vanishes. In anything, once questions and thoughts come into your mind, it all goes to pieces.

S: It seems that a pattern is all very colorless and intangible, something transparent that somehow holds all the potential within it. An illustration that comes to me is a musical scale, which is simply a set of relationships. Yet it somehow contains all of what is possible to play within that scale and has its own character. Also, a pattern is something which is almost intelligent, striving to be achieved.

JGB: I think that what you are trying to say is that the pattern is not in this world; the pattern is not the manifestation. I was talking about the "Unmanifested Sun" in the cosmology class. This is the Sun in the unconditioned world. It is colorless because it is irrelevant to talk about it having color or not. But it is the holder of the pattern of the evolution of the whole solar system, which is a much bigger and more complex thing than even the evolution of life on the earth. The visible Sun is not just the entry of the material substances, but the realisation of the pattern. But we do not see the pattern. It is the same with us— the pattern is in the unconditioned or unmanifested side of our nature but it is realised in the visible side. For the perfected man there is no gap between the two sides. <u>One way of talking about our work is that this person with body, mind, and the rest of it should be entirely integrated with the invisible side. The work can be pictured as the integration of the unmanifested and</u>

manifested. That is where trust comes in. The manifest relies by its nature on the unmanifest, but it requires a special kind of decision for the manifest to throw away the props and allow itself to be directed by something it cannot see or understand until it begins to manifest. Then one can say, "Well, that's what it's about; that's how it is."

S: How do you know when a pattern is emerging, whether it is right to let it happen or try and change it? I really get lost in this.

JGB: You know according to your own state. If you are in a subjective state you cannot have reliable indications because your state will perhaps even make you see white as black and black as white. Therefore, when it appears that something is revealing itself, it is really important to set about getting oneself as completely as possible into an objective state. If you really wish to be able to make an impartial judgement about whether something is right or not, you must be prepared to devote a certain amount of time to it. It may take you an hour. You have to put the whole thing out of your mind and concern yourself only with your own state. Supposing I had to do that—I would go and make my ablutions, sit down and do an exercise. I would certainly find that I would be tending to think about the particular thing, but I would go on until I realised that I am calmed down and no longer thinking about it. Then I would start the exercise or do a *zikr*. When I know that I am free from subjective feelings, it usually happens that the whole thing shows itself quite clearly. I need not worry about self will. One must not expect to be in the right place just because one wants to be; it does not come in that way. One has to be ready. People who work a great deal and regularly on themselves still need to prepare themselves to get into an objective state when they wish to make an impartial judgement.

S: It seemed to me that I didn't know anything about pattern until something happened and then it appeared to be inevitable. It is so extraordinary that when something happens it is as if I knew it all the time. You once said that we must be very careful never to expect anything, because if we do, we put ourselves into a different time from the one the pattern is in. I couldn't understand it then, but now I'm beginning to see that the pattern must have to do with time. It is all in the same time really, if it is in that world. I can't work out patterns for my own life but I do think that after the event one can see something.

JGB: If we are talking about pattern in the objective sense, then we don't see it because it is unmanifested. The pattern itself does not exist and therefore we cannot know it. But the pattern is that which gives existence the possibility of having the right form, being as it should be. Our task as human beings is to enable the two to fuse together so that what is happening in the manifested world really corresponds to what is happening in the unmanifested world.

In the Lord's Prayer it is said, "Thy will be done on earth, as it is in heaven." Heaven stands for the unmanifested or unconditioned world and the earth stands for the manifested or conditioned world. If we represent the *dharma* as being the will of the Father, then when we say, "Thy will be done on earth as it is in heaven," we wish that the manifested and the unmanifested should be together.

If we could know the pattern, then it would already be manifested; and if it were manifested then it would be an imperfect pattern because in manifestation something has to be lost. Therefore, the more nearly you can come to allowing the pattern to work without premeditation, without expectation, the more nearly it can come to being just right. This appears a great deal in the Gospels: trust the pattern, take no thought for the morrow. You should trust the pattern which is not manifested, not the facts which are manifested—the facts will let you down.

There is a future which is knowable because the causes of it are already here. But if you start expecting something that does not belong to the causal future, something which has a free and creative quality, you can never find it and it will never happen. By expecting a particular result—or, indeed, by expecting anything—you prevent the freer qualities from entering you.

Time and Other Worlds

S: The other day someone said that one of his daydreams was of being back in his homeland, and you said that this was not necessarily dreaming. Could you explain?

JGB: We exist in a peculiar way that has the successiveness of past, present, and future and also the peculiar property of location. We say we cannot be in two places at once or we say we cannot be in two times at once—today and yesterday, or today and tomorrow. All that is true for our physical body, as well as for any state of consciousness that is tied to a physical body. But it is not true apart from bodies.

The whole world is connected. From one way of looking at the world: *every part of it is in the same state as every other.* This way of looking is "seeing from the eternal aspect," *sub special aeternitatis.* When this way of looking operates in us we become aware of another time and another place as being here and now. We take this to be just fantasy. It can be fantasy, but it can also be a real contact. This will happen more as our inner perceptions develop. We have to be protected against it happening too much, or our experience would become unmanageable for us. When people get into this state of being detached from the present moment they are really bewildered. In the course of this Work one does lose the sense of who one is, where one is and it is very bewildering. This lasts for different periods of time according to the importance of the change that is to come.

Some people have a natural power of putting themselves into different places and times. It can also be cultivated, but one should not overcultivate it, or attach too much importance to it, because it is a secondary thing. I have this power but I do not attach importance to it. It is sometimes useful. For example, if I am asked a question about a situation, I can put myself into it and see what it is about.

When one says (about different times and places) that "it is all there," it seems to mean that everthing's fixed and determined. If the future is there and the past is there and the present moment in which I am speaking has always been there, then there isn't anything I can do except to do what I am doing or say what I am saying. When I first saw this it very much exercised my mind! It seemed to me that we were only machines. Maybe not even machines, since a machine is at least separate from something else and what I saw was simply something going on which all geared together. Some people believe that this is how it is and we call that "the mechanistic view of the world." Predicting the future is then of no value because there is nothing to be done about it.

After a certain time, I saw that this was only one way in which things are. There is also an undetermined and uncommitted world where nothing is fixed and between these two there are different kinds of worlds. *What matters to us most of all is which world we are living in.* The possibility of getting into the past or future or into some distant place does not exist in this predetermined or basic world. It only exists because there is a degree of freedom through which we can go into another world and come down again in this world at some other time or place.

Part III

Time is not of the essence. The difference between the essence and personality is that the <u>personality has no possiblity of existing at all except as a temporal process.</u> It has come into being as a temporal process. It lives as a temporal process and it cannot be any other way. And, therefore, with our personality we have no means of imagining anything else. The essence is different. It did not come into being as a process and it is not tied to time. But because the essence has not matured and developed, it cannot make use of the property that it has of not being wholly dependent on time.

Zikr

There are two traditional techniques, each of which has innumerable forms. One of these is the repitition of sounds. These repetitions are called *mantra,* sacred words, or prayers. They can be quite short, like *ram,* or complete prayers, such as the prayer of the heart introduced into the Greek Orthodox Church by St. Chrysostom. They are usually rhythmical. From time immemorial they have been used as a way of disconnecting oneself from ordinary thoughts and feelings and connecting oneself with another way of existing.

The other universal technique is breath control or the regulation of breathing. In Yoga this is called *pranayama.* Everybody knows about this, but it is often misused. All the exercises connected with breathing are concerned with strengthening our hold on a state of existence that is sometimes called the middle or intermediate state of existence, because it is between the material and the spiritual worlds. Gurdjieff spoke about breathing as providing a food for the second or intermediate body of man.

The two techniques should be used in some sort of cooperation with each other. I first saw people doing these kinds of exercises in 1919 when I went to Turkey and recognised the powerful effect that they had. I saw how Gurdjieff used these techniques and I also learnt about how Sufis, Yogis and Monks used them. But there is one particular form which I came across recently in which the two are combined in an exceptionally simple and beneficial way. I recognised that Gurdjieff had spoken about it many years ago.

You must understand that the basis for the repetition and breathing exercises is that there are energies that man needs to feed his inner life. These energies are all vibrations of different kinds in different media. Invariably all these exercises have a rhythmic quality. As it is not easy to discover an absolute rhythm, we can use a rhythm that is given to us by our bodies.

These exercises are sometimes disguised as prayers or physical activities, and sometimes they are produced involuntarily in people, like the Subud *latihan.* Sometimes they are given a definite religious or philosohical meaning like the "invocation of the name of God," Sometimes they are very complicated and even have quite elaborate rituals. The effect is the same. They bring about a transformation of energies which strengthens and liberates the finer body from the physical body. Even if we are not aware of this happening, they will produce results of this kind.

In the form I am going to introduce to you,* there is no need to have any specific ideas or to think about anything in particular. The reality is implied in the exercise and there is no need to keep one's attention on anything. You do the exercise as freely and unforcibly as possible, without trying to empty your mind or direct your thoughts. Implied in this exercise is your intention to attain to the right state of existence for yourself.

---

*Shown to Mr. Bennett by Hasan Susud. *cf.,* Bennett's autobiography *Witness,* Turnstone Press, 1975, p.366

Namaz

I will explain why I have introduced the *namaz*.* It is through this that we are able to return something of what has come to us in the course of our work during the day. It is one of our obligations to produce something, certain substances, half of which are required for our own development and the rest required for some purpose apart from or outside ourselves. This obligation has to be fulfilled. If you could understand it, it is in fact a very great part of the reason why this place* exists; and as long as this duty is being fulfilled, this place is protected and given a certain support. What we are doing through the *namaz* at the end of the day is, in effect, giving back. When someone says, "I don't feel anything from this," it is irrelevant. It is for giving and not for getting.

I do not mean that there may not be for some people a real awareness of their contact with the *Other* or a sense of unity and so on. It is right that it is so. But there are certain acts that go beyond form—for example, a religious form. They have cosmic or objective significance. They are even the same without the Sacred Image that is associated with them in tradition. There is no obligation to take part in the *namaz*. You must understand that it is not for our own benefit, but a means by which we become transmitting stations. Something is radiated from a group that does this and it will reach to where it is required. I say this to you, but you do not have to believe what I say.

*The Islamic form of prayer

**The International Academy at Sherborne House in Gloucestershire, England, where Bennett ran his school.

Meditation

We are just starting with this work on meditation. After a time some of you give up and go away. It would be good if, instead, you would persist even if you find that you have lost the thread completely. If you reach a state of maximum dispersion and helplessness in meditation—when everything is lost, your thoughts are quite uncontrollable, even your posture is difficult, when everything in you wants to stop it—it can happen that you are on the verge of a real change. From my own experience I can say that whenever I felt really helpless in meditation, but kept going, I have had most of the illuminations that have opened things for me.

You have to understand that in meditation we are not really in command: the authority is on the "other side." In the Sanskrit terminology it is the *purusha* to whom the meditation is done, not the *khestriya*.* The purusha is the other in us who is "I." It is he who is the ruler of the meditation. We cannot tell what will happen. All we can do is to put ourselves into a situation where it is possible for something to happen. In this, meditation is quite different from an exercise which depends on our will and intentional action. The only reason we take some subject for meditation is to help quiet the mind. It can happen that we have an illumination precisely connected with the subject of meditation but it can also happen in quite another direction.

It is easier to sustain the meditation by means of chanting or even by a silent mantra, but if we are patient and persist in meditation based on a question we will come to what is called

---

*Roughly speaking the *purusha* is the spirit or will, and *khestriya* the body or existence.

the *nirvikalpa samadhi*. This leads us directly to the awakening of the higher part of the self in us.* I cannot promise anyone when and how this will happen, but do not underestimate its importance. That is why I have been sorry to see people get up and leave when they have felt it impossible to continue.

S: I wonder if you could explain the difference between the morning exercise of the collected state and meditation.

JGB: They are the two extremes. In meditation you make no attempt to struggle with your thoughts or to hold your attention anywhere. If you are meditating on some theme you just direct your intention. If you are meditating with the help of a mantra, or if you are meditating on some natural process like breathing, you just put your attention in that way and you do not attempt to struggle. If your mind wanders you do not attempt to bring it back. When it comes back by itself that is good enough. In general in meditation our attention is on some specific object: a mantra, a theme, an idea or a state. If this is rightly chosen it is of such a kind as a produce in us an attraction in depth (*jazba*) and we are drawn towards a deeper part of our being.

The collected state exercise is totally different. It is just the opposite. There is no specific object. But there is the need for constant effort. It is a determined effort of one's attention to keep oneself here and now and not let anything escape. I have said that if one finds that one has, in fact, wandered, one should not get disturbed. This is a general recommendation: one cannot do deep work in oneself if one is emotionally disturbed or anxious; one must be at peace with oneself.

It is not even right to say that meditation leads to the same thing as the collected state. It does not. The real objective in meditation is to awaken different kinds of perception in us. The inner "eye," the inner awareness, is awakened by it. But the collected state exercise is an action on our own being. It enables us, for a time, to be as we should be; and therefore to allow our inner *kesdjan* body to settle down and gain more coherence.

In general one can say that exercises are active and meditation passive. Both are necessary. If one tries to go by the way of meditation alone one will become lopsided. If one tries to go by the way of exercises one will become lopsided.

*The traditional explanation is that *nirvikalpa samadhi* is the highest state of *samadhi* in which all self-consciousness disappears.

Meditation And Timelessness

Somebody asked about the blackout that can occur in meditation or exercises when there is an hiatus or gap in consciousness. There are various ways in which there can be an interruption of consciousness. There can be simply a wandering of attention. One starts thinking about breakfast or some other association comes along. This is just wandering of the mind. It means that instead of being in the exercise we are in the superficial layer of our personality.

It also happens that we simply go to sleep—one hears a gentle snoring from the corner. Sometimes one does not wake up until people begin to move about. The mind is not wandering; one is sleeping as one might in bed and one can even dream.

Everyone knows these two ways of losing contact. The third kind is what I call the *hiatus.* There is an actual break in consciousness—a blackout—where one just disappears and then comes back again. One of the things that characterises it is that one does not know how long it lasts—whether one has gone for a second, a minute or half an hour. Sometimes the hiatus is literally just for a second and yet when one comes back it might have been any length of time.

This is trance. It is called in Sanskrit *samadhi* and in Arabic *sushupti.*

In meditation there are three parts: *dharana, dhyana* and *samadhi.** The *dhyana* is meditation, or where we allow the

---

*These are the Sanskrit terms. *Dharana* is setting-up, cultivating a corresponding attitude of mind. *Dhyana* is the same as the Buddhist *jhana* and has various stages. *Samadhi* is direct absorption into the higher.

meditation to take hold of us, where we start with an image or mantra and allow it to take us over and bring us to a state of quietness. In the fourth *dhyana* there is consciousness with no thought at all. But one can sometimes slip beyond that into *samadhi.*

One can come out of *samadhi* in three ways. One can, first of all, come out exactly where one entered. In that case one is still sitting just where one is and one does not know how long it lasted or what happened. It is a real hiatus or break in consciousness. We just went out and came in again. Sometimes one is transported to another place. One finds oneself somewhere else and has to shake oneself and ask, "But where am I?" and realise "Here am I in this body."

Another way of coming out of *samadhi* is when *samadhi* passes into sleep. You wake up from this sleep and although you know you were asleep you also know that it was not ordinary sleep.

What does *samadhi* really mean? It means going out of time into eternity, out of time into timelessness. This is what we call death. In Sanskrit it is called *maha samadhi.** Gurdjieff called it the *sacred rascooarno.* Instead of being in what we call the stream of time we have moved in another direction out of time and time stops for us. The Shivapura Baba (who lived to be 136 years old) used to spend a certain amount of every day in this state. If one knows how to do this, it is one of the secrets of prolonging life. From the outside it looks like suspended animation. A person who really goes out of time may even have his bodily functions suspended. He stops breathing and his body becomes cold. When it is finished, these functions start again and people are a little disconcerted!

Between the ordinary waking state—when we are aware only of the present moment—and the state of full *samadhi,* there are various intermediate stages where our sense of time changes and we acquire the freedom to choose.

The difficulty in understanding timelessness is that what we can get hold of, what we can observe and think about, has all got a time-like character. When we slip into this other state, the

*Literally means "great samadhi."

state of timelessness, there is nothing that we can get hold of. As you become more experienced and this *samadhi* begins to be something that comes to you in your exercise or meditation, you will find that there is a state of consciousness in which one can be in *samadhi* and at the same time know things. Then you know things quite different from ordinary knowledge. A lot of this is described in the *Pali Pitikas** in terms of various kinds of perception. It is presented in a formal way as if these perceptions happened one after the other. It is very interesting and the descriptions have been of enormous help to me.

The peculiar thing abut entering other worlds is that different times are present together. Time acquires a much richer content. We really have to learn how to live in more than one world.

---

*The basic texts of Hinayana Buddhism compiled c.80 B.C. in Ceylon. Hinayana ("the lesser vehicle") Buddhism was developed by monks and geared to monastic life.

Mantra

S: In the meditation we are asked to concentrate on certain words. This is impossible for me. Perhaps this is because I can't get the meaning of the words, and after a time I can't even remember how to pronounce them or how they sound.

JGB: The words must be transferred to the heart. It is actually the prayer of the heart. The words must be vibrating in the breast. That is why it has to be done with the breath. You have to get the vibration of words into the breast and actually feel them. Of course, then the breath is necessarily lengthened; and part of the reason for having the words is to slow the breath down.

The practical problem in meditation is how to keep the words or their vibrations going without one's attention being involved in it. My way of speaking about this is in terms of the four *dhyanas* or stages of meditation. The use of a mantra or sacred word—or the colour green or anything that you like—only belongs to the first *dhyana,* but it is not wise to think that one can jump over it and go straight to the second *dhyana* where the mind remains active but there is no mental image that one holds on to. "Transcendental meditation" perhaps stands for the *dhyanas.* I spoke about this with the Maharishi Maheshyogi and he said, "Yes, that is how it is." A mantra is only the support for the first stage when you allow yourself to be carried deeper until it remains only as a vibration. When it goes deeper there is just a general state of awareness and then beyond that illumination starts—probably with the opening of what the Buddhists call *dibbha chakku**.The Maharishi always spoke of cosmic con-

*The word *chakku* (eye) is very much like the word *center* as used by Gurdjieff in talking about the "higher intellectual center" and the "higher emotional center". *Dibbha chakku* means "divine eye."

sciousness as a preliminary stage. Similarly, in Buddhism, in the deeper level, there appear "infinite space," "infinite consciousness," "nothingness," and the last *dhyana* of "neither perception nor non-perception."

Even though the language of those who teach meditation is very different, their descriptions come out to be remarkably alike because they are based on real experience.

When you do the meditation, the words should not be in your head—that is no good. The vibration must be in the breast. If you find your attention *is* in your breast and yet you are losing contact with the words, this does not matter; you are passing from the first to the second *dhyana*. The words are used to keep you away from mental associations and occupy your attention with something. If the word goes and your associations return, you are back in the superficial part of the mind and it is better to resume the words or mantra.

Collected State

S: At the end of *Beelzebub's Tales,* Beelzebub says that his method for making men right again would be to insert an organ that would make them aware of death. You said that, if you were asked, you would say to allow man to see his *kesdjan* body Is there any way in which we can become aware of the state of our *kesdjan* body?

JGB: It is said that the aim of meditation is the awakening of the *dibbha chakku,* the "third eye." The exercise that we are doing now has also a great deal to do with this. It is my own conclusion, after studying for many years what happens to people when they follow this work that they can relatively soon begin to develop these higher perceptions and can do so safely. Other people have a different view. They say that one has to do a great deal more preparation, get one's ordinary functions into order and learn how to deal with negative states and obstacles. Some even say that one should never open the higher centers until the force of negative emotions has been very greatly diminished. Certainly, some diminution is needed. That is why we did the work with the sacred impulses and I have emphasised the importance of working against like and dislike, because it is the straight way of liberating oneself to a great extent from the negative emotions. Some things that are negative are only so because of our identification, such as fear and anger and all that. There has to be some foundation laid. But my aim here has been to bring people very quickly to the development of the higher perceptions.

One way of being aware of one's *kesdjan* body is to set oneself to be perfectly still, to bring the collected state to a state of complete stillness. Then one becomes aware that one is in a different vehicle, some different body, and one can see for oneself how incoherent it is. Sometimes one can become aware of the defects in it—where it is distorted and exaggerated, and where it is weak and almost dead.

I don't say that you can do this at this moment. But it can happen that things go so well that you really do become quiet in a way you've never known before. Then you begin to see things. It is no use giving people this as an exercise, because it is not in our power to produce this complete stillness. But sometimes if we are working on the collected state a spiritual power can come and take it in hand and make us perfectly still.

Presence of God

S: It's very hard for me to say, but it's about the feeling I have about what God is, or the Higher Powers, and I find I don't know whether I just get emotional.

JGB: What is?

S: Well, I don't know. I get to the point where I think I understand. . .

JGB: I would like to say something, but I need a starting point. When you use the word 'God' can you in any way say what you mean?

S: Couldn't it be lots of things, like a force, some sort of creative power, a spirit?

JGB: Let's take a simple illustration. You can't look at the Sun at midday. It would blind you. And yet all the time you are seeing the Sun; it is in everything you look at. When you look round what you see is something done by the sunlight. You can take a piece of coloured glass and this will make it possible to look at the Sun. You will see a round red or round blue something. Or it may be that the Sun shines through a chink in the window and you see its image thrown on the wall. All kinds of things are happening because the Sun is there but the one thing you can't do is to look straight at the Sun. Is it that kind of thing?

S: Yes. It's just that I have so much feeling about it that I don't know whether I'm being over-sensitive.

JGB: Ask yourself, what does all this feeling do for you? With this, are you able to face all the ups and downs of life? Do you remember when you need to?

You spoke about a creative spirit. Let us say that there is something or other that has an action. We can call it some kind of energy or some kind of spiritual power. I can say, "Yes, there really is such a thing, this is true." And then you say that you become sensitive to it and you have something deeply stirred up in you. Yes, that is true. But you can also lose a lot of energy—not only *that* energy, but some of your own if it begins to catch you emotionally. You must ask yourself, "What is it that I do better because of this? Am I better able to manage my life? Am I able to manage my own thoughts and emotional states?" If so, then you can be sure it is a good thing. But if it only disturbs you, excites you, or fills you with some kind of energy that takes your attention away from what you have to do, then it is not a good thing. In the list of the sort of things that are the gifts of the spirit, peace is given right at the beginning. If there is a spiritual action that is right, one of the tests of its rightness is that it produces a state of peace in us and not a state of turmoil and disturbance.

Personality Work - Essence Work

JGB: The words are very simple: essence work, personality work. The active force is in personality, the denying force in the body. We start with this: I and my body. "I will make my body do this," is the beginning of some separation and some kind of work, *but the "I" does not mean anything except personality.* It is possible to get stuck there and take this as work. Self-will grows stronger by it. It is not only with the body. Someone I knew set himself not to justify. He had heard not justifying was very good and he set himself that whatever he did he would never justify and never explain. He succeeded, but it was still in his personality.

My great concern with all of you who are capable of making efforts and struggling with yourselves is that it should get from personality to essence. You see, this is the most difficult thing. You may struggle with your body. Personality is affirming and the body denying. Then you have something in you that sees that this is strengthening the wrong part of you. You cease making the effort. Then it is essence affirming and personality denying; but it is difficult to be really sure that it is not the body suddenly becoming affirming with a beautiful excuse!

We must listen to people very carefully when they speak about it, because we are all listening from our personalities. We have to put ourselves into the position of what was actually being done, not what is said about it.

The "mesoteric" stage of the work consists in transferring the affirmation from personality to essence. You can tell for yourself that this is beginning to happen when there is an awareness that something in you is really seeing, which is not only separate from what is being done, but has *authority.* This is very different from the helpless seeing you can have that just looks on when you are doing something foolish.

In Buddhism, *seeing* is referred to in many ways. There are, for example, three "eyes," The *dhamma chakku,* or the "eye for the truth" is much like Gurdjieff's magnetic center. Then there is the "divine eye," the *dibbha chakku** and one beyond that, which is probably the same as the higher intellectual center.

What we are looking for in the mesoteric stage is a kind of self-seeing that has authority and the power to tell the personality to stop. It is a very hard thing. I have seen so many people go on year after year doing their personality work saying, "I and my body," "I and my negative emotions," "I and my attention," when all the time this "I" is just personality. Even if one sees that this is all it is, even if one is quite devastated by realizing that the whole thing is a fake and the "I" that is making the efforts is simply feeding itself on the work, this will not change things.

In Ouspensky's book *In Search of the Miraculous,* he shows a series of diagrams illustrating the inter-relation of essence, personality, many I's and so on, and how the initiative can change in the way I have been talking about. When I first heard about this many years ago it was nothing but words. Now I see how it is. For the sleeping man, something gets his attention or interest and there resides the affirmation. His personality plays that role passively and essence does not come into it. Then it can change over and the personality becomes active. This is the first stage in the work. Then the essence begins to wake up and the personality becomes the denying force. This is the important stage to reach. There is no direct way of doing it because the personality intercepts it the whole time. It has to come indirectly by all kinds of things that bring some consciousness, some independence and some power into the essence.

S: I sometimes see something, then feel it getting spoilt by myself.

---

*Possibly, the higher emotional center.

JGB: We see something and then something starts to go on in us, some kind of reasoning. Now, <u>essence does not reason.</u> How can we be in essence? *ESSENCE KNOWS~ AT A GUT LEVEL. ESSENCE DOES NOT NEED TO REASON ‑*

Can this be done by wishing? This is a likely thing to keep it right, but in order to speak about this one must put oneself into the situation. You must give some time to do that. . .

And I saw myself as separate, just watching what was happening. I saw that it was possible for me to draw back and let my personality go on. It was doing quite intelligently, thinking the right kind of things and so on. But all this was outside—I could make it so—and I remained not doing anything at all, not even wishing. If you are able to cultivate this capacity for remaining unmoved in some place in you, so that you have part of your attention in the consciousness that you are not thinking, not feeling, not wishing, not even being anything—then in some way what is required reveals itself to you. You are no longer thinking, but the required ideas, or the required states, just present themselves to you.

S: If one wakes up in the middle of an activity, would doing the *zikr* help to transfer the experience or hold it?

JGB: It helps, but what the result will be must be put out of your mind. If something happens to you so that you become aware of yourself as objective (seeing yourself from outside) and the thought of doing the *zikr* comes, then certainly do the *zikr*. This is the sort of thing I was just talking about, for if you can keep yourself in the right state of separation, what has to be done or thought presents itself to you. More often than not the action precedes the thought, you find yourself doing the thing that is required.

Is it possible for us to bring the work from personality into essence? This is the *fana-i akham**, when you stop believing in the personality, when you see that it is just a mask that you are wearing and it is not you. It is to see that and accept it entirely. All the stuff that has been acquired in the course of your life re-

---

*akham comes from *hukum*, being under laws, conditioned. The *fana-i akham* is here the annihilation of attachment to conditioned existence, to personality, the man machine. *cf.*, J.G. Bennett, *Deeper Man*, Turnstone Press, 1978, pp. 231-2

mains not you. You have to be able to live with it as you live with a suit of clothes that provides a necessary covering. Personality is a necessary covering, a means of presenting oneself to other people and for dealing with the world. But it is not you. *Not to identify with it.* You have to see that this person who is thinking, feeling, talking and so on is an artificial thing.

To realise this is very difficult. However much I talk about it I would regard it as wonderful if there were three or four people here who could really see it.

It does happen that one can see it *and not be aware that one has seen it.* This is sometimes a valuable safeguard, because if you become aware that you have seen it you get caught back into it again; you then think you are free when once again you are in the middle of it all. You have to set yourselves to remain in a state of seeing.

Let us say your personality is offended or distressed or in some way agitated. How do we become aware that this distress and offence is not ourselves—that it is the personality reacting in this way? The personality may be checking itself, it may be behaving in a very discreet way, harbouring a resentment and not showing it outwardly—but this can be just a kind of play acting. The personality is tempted to think, "I am controlling my state, I am not manifesting anger or resentment," and it really believes it has achieved a separation. Then comes a moment of light, when you see that the whole thing is a play and you want nothing of it. What really matters to us is revealed to that seeing one in us. So long as it can remain detached, it is able to receive illumination. Also, it is not without power. Its presence changes everything. It can even have authority and it should have authority.

We must remember all the time that our personality can simulate all this. We can have the feeling of self-control, of right behavior, right attitudes and even—especially—of making efforts and doing work. Yet it is all within the personality and we do not see it at the time. Perhaps afterwards we notice that we are pleased with ourselves, that somehow we think we have achieved something and we are comparing ourselves to others. Then the whole pretense is laid bare. It was all just to feed our own egoism.

Then we become distressed and think, "Is there any real Work at all? If even my efforts, my attempts at self-observation, my sincerity with myself all turns out to be just play acting in my personality, is there anything?" As long as one is like that there is still no freedom, because it is simply another part of the personality in a state of distress. And then the real *djartklom** occurs and one sees it all; there is no longer any distress, no longer any disturbance, because one knows that this is not what matters.

S: If you can remain at the point of seeing, then there is this extraordinary thing that occurs. What you need is put in front of you. And then life is so simple. When it happened to me I felt quite extraordinary.

JGB: That is the mark by which one recognises—it is so.

S: But for most of the time the personality problem is terrifically strong at that point.

JGB: I remember a story of Ubaidallah Ahrar**-who, as you probably know, is one of my great heroes, and who I can never think of without feeling myself present with him. When he was a young man, he had extraordinary powers in the domain of *hanbledzoin.*** He and another dervish were in the market place of Bukhara. I must explain that the great sport of central Asia was, and still is, wrestling. It was combined with gambling, a real vice with them. There were two wrestlers, one a big burly strong enormous man and the other a much weaker one. The big man was beating up the other one. Ubaidallah Ahrar said to his companion, "Let's help here," and they concentrated their *hanbledzoin.* The weak wrestler had an enormous surge of

*Term invented by Gurdjieff to designate the separation of the three forces (active, denying and reconciling) in which the reality of the present moment can be restored, *cf.*, J.G. Bennett, *Talks on Beelzebub's Tales,* Coombe Springs Press, 1977, *Djartklom.*

**Ahrar lived in the 16th century and was one of the last and greatest of the *Khwajagan,* the Masters of Wisdom of Central Asia. *cf.*, *Masters of Wisdom,* J.G. Bennett, Turnstone Press, 1977.

***Term invented by Gurdjieff to designate, roughly speaking, the inner blood or "blood of the soul" of man.

energy and went and picked up the big man, threw him over his head, stunned him and so on. There was great excitement in the crowd! Ubaidallah Ahrar noticed his friend was still concentrating his energy and said, "That's enough."

This story occurred to me as a picture—and maybe it was really intended as a parable—of how the personality and essence are. Personality is the great big wrestler who always wins. But sometimes the weak one, the essence, gets an inflatus of energy from somewhere or other and an impossible thing happens. Personality is stopped dead in its tracks and can't do anything. You find yourself doing the exact opposite of what you wanted to do or intended to do and which your whole personality thought was irresistable. You wonder how it happens. If you are honest with yourself you know you did not do it; this other thing came from somewhere which turned it upside down. It is a great thing to learn how to call for this when it is needed. Before that is possible one must be able to see one's personality as something alien, and also that there is something in us which makes it almost impossible to avoid slipping back into it. A moment of inattention, or a moment of self-lovingness and one is back to the state of the personality aping it all. It is saying all the right things but now the whole thing is a cheat.

The Shivapuri Baba told me a story about himself. He was up in the Shivapuri Hills and the thought came to him that *he* had achieved liberation and come to knowledge of God; that he was able to see the reality of things and how wonderful that was. At that moment he was struck by a bolt of lightning, his hair turned white and he entered *djartklom*. He saw that he hadn't done any of it at all. At that time he was 112 years old and his hair was still black and he had flaming eyes—I have a picture of him taken like that. He lived for another 30 years or so but never again did he think, "How wonderful I am." Not everyone can merit that kind of *djartklom*—when Jove himself sends his thunder!

Hanbledzoin

S: You said something about those two fellows directing *hanbledzoin* on some wrestlers. How do you do that? Providing you have some.

JGB: They were very young, you know. They learnt better later on. They were exceptional. Ubaidallah Ahrar was an extraordinary man and he had extraordinary powers from childhood. Gurdjieff also had this power and he used to play about with it in the same sort of way. But he gave up doing it, unless there was a definite reason for helping people. Yes, you have to learn how to do it. I'm always watching to see when it is possible for me to teach certain things which I would like to teach you.

Part IV

Dance is used not only for making bodily expressions but also for expressing beliefs and laws. It can be used for recalling the past and for preparing the future. There are various traditional ways of expressing the history of a people through dancing. There are initiatory rituals that prepare results that will be met within the future. This great science of the use of the human body as an instrument is really much neglected in our time . We use it in various specialized ways—for entertainment, for sport, for sexual stimulation—but the real deeper uses are being lost. It is fortunate for us that Gurdjieff and the group of people who saw the importance of dance spent years visiting different parts of the world collecting and recording what they found in the way of all these uses of the body. Gurdjieff, himself, attached so much importance to this work that when he was choosing a descriptive title for himself he said, "I think the best is to call myself a teacher of temple dancing."

Mystery of the Human Body

Suppose there were other presences in the room—spirits or ghosts—that do not have bodies like ours. We would not be aware of them, or hardly at all. We are aware that we are together because we are aware of our bodies.

But what is a human body? I say, "my body." If you stop to look at this "my body" you will see that it is a strange way to speak. Who is the "me" to whom this body belongs? I am talking as if there were two distinct things: the "me" and the body which "belongs to me" which I own in some way like I own a watch or a pair of shoes.

We seldom stop to notice what a strange idea this is. If this is my body, what am I doing with it? How often is it really my body, in the sense that I am aware of it belonging to me, and that it is "I" that am using it? If we watch, we can see how much our body lives its own life. It is really as if there were two different things. One is this body which goes about its business and the other is "me" who sometimes remembers this body. For the most part "me" lets "it" do its own work—as "it" is speaking for me now, producing sounds or vibrations, which you are hearing.

We are not accustomed to ask questions which are not taught us at school. Soon we stop asking questions and therefore stop noticing that the world is very strange and the way we exist is also strange. Maybe children are aware of this strangeness. Their questions show that they notice that it is strange, but we forget all that. But if we want to live full lives, we must ask these questions and be determined to find answers. For example; "What do I mean when I say 'my body'?"

If we pursued that question with a determination to understand what it really means we would go a long way. We would find ourselves getting out of our depth. How are we sure that we ought not to be saying, "This body is me?" Why should I be so sure that I am the one that owns the body and not the body that owns me? How often am I doing what my body wants and not what I want?

The human body is a mystery. It is very obvious that there is a body. We do not ask ourselves whether a body is a possession that we have somehow acquired or who it is that could have "acquired" it. And we do not know the answer. All that we know is that our experience is in some way linked to this body. To say that we "have" a body is to make a division between that which has the body and the body that is possessed. We do not know what this means. Let us just accept that in people there are at least two distinct components—one the bodily and the other the spiritual nature. Let us go further and accept that the spiritual nature did not arise out of the bodily nature. Since we know in a tangible way that the body is made out of the materials of the earth, we can also say that the body does not arise out of the spiritual nature.

The mystery is how these two come together. It is what is meant by *the squaring of the circle.* The square body and the circular spirit are very different, yet they are together. We speak about this as "incarnation" for the spirit is entering into the flesh. Is it possible to say anything more? The body is evidently conditioned and limited and, in some way, an unconditioned and unlimited "something" has come to be associated with it. This is why I compare it to squaring the circle, where there will always be something left over that does not fit. Looked at in this way we should be saying not that we have a body, but that the body is *imposed* on us. We have been fitted into a body. In order to clip our wings, to condition us, and see to it that we remain in this conditioned state of existence in the material world, the body has been imposed to restrict and restrain us. We can only see what this inadequate visual instrument allows us to see—a minute fraction of the radiations that exist. There are radiations that pass through walls which it would be useful to experience, but we cannot. The same applies to all our senses. All sense perception is a conditioning, limited thing, a shutting out rather that a letting in. We are prevented from seeing too much.

The human brain also, though enormously complex, is only able to provide us with the most ludicrously simplified pictures of the world. Nearly the whole of the wealth of experience of the world is shut out by the limitation of the brain.

The body is condemned to wear out. Under ideal conditions, it could last for three or four hundred years, but it rarely lasts for more than a hundred. Through this simple knowledge we can begin to form a picture of the restrictive character of existence in this body. Compared with the restrictions we do not know about, because our body has entirely shut us off from possible modes of experience quite incomprehensible in terms of this bodily existence, such restrictions are nothing.

Why has our spiritual nature been captured and confined in this box? It has not been done to the animals. They are simple things with their fixed feelings, perceptions and inner world and they lack the peculiar conflict of natures that is latent in every man—the conflict between the concealed sense of his own unlimitedness and the only too obvious prison of his bodily limitations. Why are we put into a condition so incompatible with what we really feel to be ourselves?

Manifestation

The body is a means of transforming energies. In a simple way this is done through eating food so we can supply our bodies, our feelings, and our minds with energies they need. There is a great deal to be learned about the nourishment of our higher powers through breathing and the control of energies through rhythm. Everyone knows the role that posture plays in Yoga, which produces specific effects on the different centers of the body known as the *chakras.* There is an immense science of the human body and its potential for experience and expression, its transformation of energies and its use as an instrument of perception and cognition. There is also the use of the human body in sharing experience with others, which we call *manifestation.*

At this moment I am using my body to communicate with you and you are using your bodies to communicate with me through the limited and restrictive processes of the production and hearing and interpretation of speech sounds. If I have an inner vision of what the human body really represents there is no means by which I can communicate this to you by means of speech sounds. Yet what else have we between us?

In reality, man is not confined to speech for manifestation. All his works are manifestations: every movement, every gesture, every act of his body. The whole significance of this is lost to us because we seldom, and with much difficulty, manifest consciously from our own intention and nearly always react simply as part of the process of energy transformation which we share with everything else. If we are incarnated in this body for the purpose of bringing something of the spiritual world into the material world—and maybe of restoring something of the physical world to the spiritual one—then our manifestations are a cosmic necessity. In this there is a corresponding reponsibility. If I, because I am a man, am able to manifest in a different way from what is possible for an animal, am I fulfilling my human destiny? How far and how often am I doing things that an animal cannot do?

We are accustomed, and have been for a long time, to associate the manifestation of our spiritual or intelligent nature with speech. We assume that we express ourselves through speech in a deeper and more significant way than through walking or touching. But why should we suppose that speech has this specially significant character? We know that speech is dependent on other things for its effectiveness, such as the quality of the speech sounds. For those who intend to influence people and touch their emotions, nearly always speech is accompanied by gesture. This itself is a recognition that even the speech sound is not a complete communication. And we know that works of art have a power to influence which is both more lasting and stronger than nearly all speech.

Through dance and mime the body can produce a transient but powerful effect upon people. By certain sympathetic characteristics of the body, one body is able to respond to the movements of another and receive experiences that are transmitted by unconscious imitation. Here is a tremendous potential for communication. When speech was a more transient instrument than it is today, when there was no means of writing and recording speech, its transience was compensated by the use of repetitive self-reproducing manifestations such as rituals, dances, and ways of carrying out the ordinary operations of life.

A picture comes into my mind of women weaving in Nepal, where they have only a row of sticks in a field and move with their skeins around them. They have no loom, nothing but their own bodies. The way in which they move their bodies is transmitted to the pattern of the cloth. This is a very ancient thing from before the time that looms were invented. I remember seeing people making rush matting with three or even four generations together—an old, old, man with his son and grandchildren all sitting together weaving. I could see that this was a continuous process that had been going on for thousands of years in a way that could not be transmitted by speech. There are village dances such as those of Greece and Persia which have continued for a very long time as a means of manifesting and transmitting certain kinds of experiences and sustaining certain activites or practical work. I have seen Africans hoeing the fields in lines all singing together in rhythm, making an indescribably beautiful pattern of movement.

These things are very ancient and they have played a great part in the preservation of cultures. They have been used to preserve and transmit knowledge that cannot readily be expressed in words, particularly knowledge connected with the mysteries of manifestation; that is, the way in which the world fulfills its destiny. People have despaired of doing this with words without spoiling it. But to do it through ritual the body has to be used in a special way. It has to be *deconditioned* to be able to be something nearer to an instrument corresponding to the spiritual nature of man. This is a difficult thing.

One must understand that the ancient use of dance and ritual belonged to periods which had a deeper concern with the spiritual nature of man than our own. At this time, we are almost exclusively concerned with the conditioned nature of man and therefore we have no time to concern ourselves with the spiritual nature. The thought of spending three or four hours every day in developing our capacity for manifesting would be totally unacceptable in the conditions of modern life. At this time, the only people who train the body to produce manifestations, do so in order to produce an effect upon people. Sacred dances often demand the opposite: the dancers must withdraw into themselves and produce the minimum of emanations and it is for the people watching to penetrate into the movement from within and not from the outside. Such dances are the opposite of spectacles.

Now let us look at sacred dancing and all the various actions that are connected with it. First of all there is the action that is for development, preparation and training. Temple dancers, whether men or priestesses, have more severe preparation than almost any other kind of vocation. It may take ten or fifteen years of preparation to be accepted as a temple dancer in some

Eastern sanctuaries and temples, and training starts in very early childhood.

Dances are used also for training adults, to release them from various tensions and habits, develop their attention and for other things. In the course of this training the students or novices learn how to use the dance to produce various mental and emotional states in themselves and how to combine them. They learn how to set themselves free from their own bodily activity, so that they can fulfill the precept: action without attachment, or acting without concern for the fruits of action. The strength of the body and its powers of endurance have to be developed also.

Properly speaking, temple dancing (or sacred dancing or ritual dancing) is not a private affair, it is for sharing. Sacred dances convey certain beliefs and truths and transmit various kinds of energies to people. There are the healing therapeutic dances, where the dancer is able (by his own movements) to transmit energy to sick people. This science was well known in Africa and is only now being lost. It is also known in certain parts of Central Asia. This is all part of the second stage of the use of the body, that is, as a means of manifestation to others. In ancient times, particularly before the discovery of writing, dance was used as a means of transmitting certain knowledge from generation to generation, because dances can be preserved over a long period of time. We can see that our own Morris dancing has been preserved over a long period of time. Wise men of ancient times used dance and ritual as a means of recording their understanding of the laws of the world. Some later generation could then decipher them, as we decipher a book in some lost language. And when in fact we decipher some of the ancient languages, such as the cuneiform or the hieroglyphic, we come to realise how much people knew thousands of years ago which was subsequently lost. The same is true for the dance.

The innermost use of the dance is where it is not for oneself, as in one's own training and development, nor for others, where it is for manifestation and transmission, but an act of worship. One dances for God, or for the Sacred Image in which one believes. When the dance is in this form it is truly sacred and lifts people into communion. This is the purpose of it. It is not simply homage, made from one being to another, as one might dance in front of a king; it is different from that. For example, one of the greatest exponents of the sacred dance was Jallal ad-din Rumi, the great Persian poet and mystic, for he said that through the dance (the *sama*) he entered into direct communion with God. I have met Dervishes who are followers of his—now many centuries after Rumi—who assured me that when they do the *sama* they feel themselves to be united with him and feel as if they become him and he becomes them. Mystical union is part of the higher significance of dancing.

We work with dances and exercises that are derived from Gurdjieff. They were all collected by him in the East and he told us their sources. By far the greater part of them comes from central Asia or eastern Turkestan, that is the region from Tashkent, through the valleys of the Amu Darya and up to the oases of the Gobi desert and eastern and north eastern Afghanistan. That is a region where, about a thousand years ago, there was another very remarkable man who collected and preserved a great deal of knowledge of the sacred rituals, Ahmad Yasawi.*

*cf., *Masters of Wisdom*, J.G. Bennett, Turnstone Press, 1977, pp. 128-9 and 150-1.

Ritualistic Movements

Every ritual is a manifestation and every kind of shared religious experience involves some kind of ritual. The body is also used in the representation of higher historical events (or cosmic laws) through gestures and movements. In these situations the spectator should not be passive, but a participant. That is why you who have come to see the movements have been encouraged to work at them yourselves, so that you will not be outside the experience, looking on, separated from the performers. There should be the same kind of sharing as when we sit together in silence.

I will say something about some of the more ritualistic movements that you will see. First of all, the *Assyrian Mourners* belongs to a tradition that goes back a very long time, to the time when the attitude to death was very different from what it is now. It was then understood that those who had been bereaved should not grieve for the dead, because this produces suffering for the dead people and they are held back. Professional mourners were employed, but their task was to remind the dead of the need to leave the body, to draw them away from attachment to the earth. You will see gestures which directly express this. Then, amongst several dances taken from Tibet, we have the *Tibetan Masks*. Originally, the dancers would have been equipped with fantastic masks and costumes that flail as they move. The object was to draw the satanical forces towards oneself in order to neutralise them by one's own energy and remove their harm for others.

We shall finish with the *Great Prayer*. This requires some explanation, because it represents the entire pilgrimage of the soul until final enlightenment. It begins with the priests and priestesses kneeling on the floor. They develop in their minds' eye from the moment of birth, to the awakening of perception and the powers of the body, and then the opening of the emotional life and the intellectual life. The whole movement depicts four stages of renunciation or disillusionment, that in Sufism are called fana—annihilation. The first is disillusionment with the visible world: realising that the world is impermanent and will not provide an answer to one's questions. This ends with a prostration which signifies commitment to follow the Way. In Gurdjieff's terminology, this is the stage of man number four. The second is disillusionment with one's outer self or personality. You will see gestures which depict aspects of self belief. With the second prostration, there is death and resurrection, and there rises the man of the soul who is liberated from this world. He becomes the perfected man who has what in Buddhist terminology is called "the spotless eye of the truth" because he has the ability to know what is right—all of which is represented by the gestures. Then comes the great renunciation, the renunciation of one's own egoism. Man becomes the bodhisattva or compassionate one. After the third prostration, there is depicted an action for the salvation of others. He turns towards the four cardinal points offering himself to the world to help all creatures. Finally, God takes over and man comes to the state of final death and liberation. Some other power is taking possession, but each of the gestures is made by conscious intention and the renunciation is truly conscious. The final death is represented by the priests and priestesses curled up in the position of the unborn child. When they rise, God has been born in their souls and only God is present. In Buddhism, this is the stage of the final enlightenment, when the earth trembles. We return to the original gestures and then there is silence.

Doing Movements

JGB: I happened to be in Paris a lot at the time when Gurd-jieff was putting Number 17* together. Even with his extraor-dinary capacity for mental imagery and after long years of experience, he worked very hard at it. This made me under-stand how much is involved in some of these movements.

I know from experience the extraordinary feeling that comes of actually being in a different world when, even for half a minute, one does a movement *rightly*. It is the same for the singer or in-strumentalist. There is a moment when one knows that one is doing it exactly right. One must not accept anything less than this. In the movements you have a marvellous thing. You must be able to see for yourself that the kind of thinking in words and pictures that goes on in the so-called mind is totally useless for you. You should be thankful that you are put in front of a situa-tion where you just cannot get anywhere with this apparatus. The disease of formatory thinking is really a terrible disease.

S: The only time when I have a feeling that there might be something like God or Higher Powers is in the movements. Ever since the very beginning of doing the movements, I felt that I needed some help to do them and I just didn't know where to get it. I find myself saying, "God can help me," or something of that nature. It seems to help me. I only sometimes remember to give thanks for help. Only in the movements is it all linked together.

JGB: This is because you accepted the movements in a way that you did not accept other parts of the work. Everyone will be

*Number 17 is one of the series of thirty-nine movements that Gurdjieff put together just before his death. Later on, Bennett refers to Number 13 and Num-ber 24 from the same series.

different in this and it is one reason why we need such a diversity. When you accept something in the name of the work, then the work is present in it. If you treat the movements as sacred, they *are* sacred—not merely in your imagination. Through the movements this sacred power is able to reach you.

In old Russia there were very devout people, but they had a great number of beliefs that couldn't find a place in any ordinary idea of Christianity. They believed that there were spirits in forests and spirits in houses, and if one undertook something one should ask the spirit of the place to allow and help it. And life was very good, although it was very hard. These people felt that they were in connection with the spiritual world all the time—and they were. It is through this sense of the sacred being open in us that we can get into the world which in Sufism is called the *alam-i arvah,* the world of spirits. I have said that the spiritual power is like the Sun and that we do not see the Sun. What we see are carpets, chairs and so on—the light of the Sun reflected in these things. In some kind of way the *alam-i arvah* is a reflection of the power of God, of the Spirit. If you believe and accept that you are in that world, you really are in it. And when you accept the movements in such a way, then what one could call "the spirit of the movements" comes into what you do. It is even possible to say that every movement has its own spirit and sometimes you can feel that it is the spirit doing the movement. This does not mean that God is doing the movement—God is a long way beyond that. It means that something is at work which is not of the bodily world.

We should believe that there is a spirit world, because there is. Everything has its own spirit for which there is an invocation or prayer. Buddhism told people to be very careful not to think of God in the way that they had been doing. But it never discouraged belief in the spirits. In the sermons of Buddha, one can read of such things as the spirits of a wood being pleased because the disciples were living there and made it a sacred place. I certainly feel the presence of spirits. In the movements one can be aware of them. Number 13 has something particularly good for us in it. A moment comes with this movement when you feel as if the spirit of the movement has got into you.

There are other worlds than this bodily one and in the first is the "spirit of things," or "the essence of things." We must not be afraid of this world, and we must try not to be doubtful about it. It is contrary to the ordinary way of thinking which simply divides the world into minds without bodies, or other kinds of bodies. The "spirit of Number 13" is not some mind that is thinking of 13 or having a mental image of 13; it is something which is striving to be Number 13.

There is a marvellous expression of this in Stevenson's fable *The Poor Thing.* * Something is able to bring a man into being, yet it is nothing at all.

There are three or four movements which are special in this kind of way. *Schadze Vadze* (Number 24) for me has the feeling about it that there is something wanting a body, that wants to be able to manifest and it is looking to us to be able to manifest. If you look at the movements in this way you may gain a different attitude towards them. The movements are not just something that somebody invented in the past and put on a piece of paper to remind them what they were, or something like that. They are something that wants to come into being, wants to be flesh and blood, and when the movement is done by us then it wants to be done rightly. When it finds a body that is doing it rightly, the spirit becomes happy and you yourself feel happy.

The movement is just like the *Poor Thing* of Stevenson's fable; it wants to be clothed in a man and it has the power to attract what it needs. The movements have power and people who watch them want to be doing them, to give birth to them in themselves. If we had enough people who could do the movements really well and if it were possible to show them, it might be a very powerful way of attracting people. Almost in spite of themselves they would want to come and enter into this work.

Fables, R.L. Stevenson, Coombe Springs Press, 1975.

Part V

JGB: *What were you going to say?*

S: *I was yawning. I wasn't going to say anything.*

Affirmation and Denial

JGB: A challenge is an opportunity of making a particular kind of demand on oneself and it is this that produces the *triad* without which is not possible to have Work. This is the triad of evolution which begins from our passive force, from our denial. The passive force puts itself in front of a very precise affirmation — this is the challenge. Out of that comes the possibility of work, the *third force.* It does not come from our affirming side. The trouble is that our affirming side gets caught into our self-will so when we work from our own affirmation it is terribly difficult to do it with freedom from self-will. When we work from our own denial, it is on the whole much easier.

An affirming state is one where one feels one's own energy, that one is able to do things. One feels one has the strength to make efforts, to make demands of oneself and that one can direct this either into an effort or into satisfying one's own wishes and interests. In all these cases where the initiative is coming from one's active state, the impulse is to do something. For some purposes this is necessary and when we have an active state it has to be turned to good account. But the very nature of an active state is that it has to blend with a passive one and, eventually, it will run down.

But if we are in a passive state without energy or understanding, or in a state of bewilderment, or in a state of revolt against any demand that is being made of us, and yet we contrive in that state to put ourselves in front of an affirmation, to say, "I will do this," without feeling any motive or wish to do it, then something different is set up. Everyone who has done this knows that there is a liberation. We are free and a whole new vista opens. We must understand the necessity for this kind of action in us: to work when we cannot work and do not wish to work; when there is nothing in us that feels able to work, when everything in us wants to postpone it or make it different. This triad of evolution can and does open up a whole lot of doors and possiblitities. Immediately, we are lifted to a different level. From that, other opportunities come. It is this that is the challege in front of all life—how to raise itself from its own deny-ing state.

Awareness of the "terror of the situation," or the realisation of death of various things can awaken in us the necessity to work; but when the work comes from one's own decision without "why" then it is a pure essence triad of evolution. This takes us directly on the path towards the source of everything existing. It is the way. We must get a taste of that.

JGB: Unless we can import a value system into this whole technological complex that we have built up, we are in a bad way. One comes from one place and one comes from the other. The great awkwardness is that it is easier to get a response from the lower nature than from the higher.

S: I used to take lessons from a lady who taught politicians to speak. I used to hear her say, "Put some dynamics in your voice." I realized that sort of weight coming from the vocal ap-paratus was an imposition. The first time I heard you speak, you did not use any dynamic with your voice and this seemed very strange to me because an audience expects you to do that. When it doesn't happen, at first people do not like it because you are not imposing anything on them. I wondered if this is part of the non-imposition of will? I noticed it was the same with Hasan Susud.

JGB: As I said, it is easier to get a response from the lower nature than from the higher nature. The secret is that force always produces a reaction in the lower nature and only non-force can produce a reaction in the higher nature. But if force is constantly used, then the lower nature is constantly exercised and this is not good for anything.

The one thing that a wise man wants to avoid is finding himself transmitting the affirming force. If he has to, he has to. But if he can avoid it he does so, because he realises that this means that the force has to degenerate. If he is able, and the circumstances allow it, he should always try to transmit the third force. He should be more concerned with setting up situations and with the free response to the moments when things are possible, than with initiating and pushing and so on. But this is difficult for people to understand. It is the whole secret of the Ashiata Shiemash organisation* for man's existence.

Sometimes the taking of the active role is necessary. What you call "dynamic" is precisely where the speaker himself is transmitting the active force. He sets himself with all that he can to be active and to have the audience passive. But how much better it is when it is the other way round.

I remember an experience when Elizabeth and I went to see Pablo Casals about twenty-five years ago. We happened to see him when he was recording the Beethoven Trio with a famous Russian pianist and a very famous first violin. The pianist was determined to get the tempi the way he wanted. He would play the first movement too fast because he thought it would be more brilliant or something. Casals let him play as he liked. Each time they listened to the result he knew it was wrong. They played it at least ten times and each time Casals never once varied. He played as if nobody else were there and he played exactly the same way. Then I saw the difference between Casals and the pianist. The pianist had no idea of what to do except to put himself over as a solo artist. He obviously never thought of anything else but himself as active and the audience as passive. But never once did I hear Casals be "dynamic," never once did he impose himself on the audience in all the times that I heard him play. The end of the story is that the Trio was never recorded at all. Towards the end of a long day, Casals said, "I am tired," and that was that. The pianist could not learn the lesson of how to be an instrument of the music.

You have to get out of the way. If you are there then you will introduce the dynamism. If you are not there, then it will go through you. The things that one never forgets all one's life have that quality.

---

*A reference to a chapter in Gurdjieff's book *Beelzebub's Tales to His Grandson.*

Doing Exercises

S: What kind of energies work in the morning exercise?

JGB: The energy that is used is the sensitive energy. This is the energy that we primarily control. When we work to control thought, feeling, and sensation, it brings us into a state of receptiveness and a higher energy can come—the creative energy. We are not aware of the higher energy for it is beyond consciousness. When it comes everything works differently and there can be a great release of vital energy, so the whole body is alive and the attention can be different. But if we say we work with the sensitive energy, who are "we"? The "we" is not the sensitive energy working with itself, it is the conscious energy, which is a spiritual energy. In the exercises we are working on the boundary is between the sensitive and the conscious. It can happen that help comes from a higher energy which acts on the automatic level. Then everything goes much more clearly.*

When we are alert and attentive and keeping ourselves as near as possible to the boundary, when we really try to keep our attention inward, to get behind our thoughts, behind and behind and behind, we finally come to a place where it is blank. The boundary is like a dark space. This is the barrier between the world of form and the formless world.

S: I've had experiences of this help you describe, but it does not seem to increase my ability to follow intentions.

JGB: In order to do, there must be will. It is only the will that can decide. You can have the intention of doing something

---

*cf., J.G. Bennett, *Energies*, Coombe Springs Press, 1978. Lecture IV.

without willing it. We have to learn about decision separately and it is a special thing. Now, you say why is it that making the breakthrough into the higher energies does not make our intentions into acts of will? It simply means that the opening you have had is not sufficient. It is possible to get a very spectacular change in your state—feeling overwhelmed with energy flooding in—with a very small opening into the spiritual world. When the breakthrough is a real opening, *satori,* you can do whatever you choose. You do not have to prepare anything; everything you choose to do you have the power to do.

S: Does that mean that the break closes up again?

JGB: It closes up again, but each time it's repeated, its opening becomes easier until one is able to open it at will. I was thinking of Francis Thompson's *Hound of Heaven:*

"Yet ever and anon a trumpet sounds
From the hid battlements of Eternity;
Those shaken mists a space unsettle, then
Round the half-glimpsed turrets slowly wash again."

And he goes on to say:

"But not ere him who summoneth
I first have seen . . . ."

Seeing

S: How far do you think that concepts taken from particular areas are reliable tools for creating a cosmology or general system?

JGB: Do you mean something like the scheme of energies?

S: Yes; the concept of energies works in dealing with matter. It is quite easy to believe in a notion of materiality before it comes from experience. It has been said that the system is more materialistic than materialism. Do you think that the use of the term "energy" is a bit ambiguous at times?

JGB: Gurdjieff said many things to shock and disturb. Not only, "more materialistic than materialism," but also that, "the Work is against Nature and against God." You have to see what he means; you have to understand about evolution and involution. He is talking in the same sense as the story of Jacob's struggle with the angel in *Genesis*. It is necessary to struggle with the force which is coming out of the Source. In order to go up the stream, you have to swim against the stream. If the stream is called "good" then the swimming against the stream must be "bad," but this is obviously *facon de parler*. The irrigation of the plains depends upon the streams coming down the mountains. In the same way the world is maintained and created by the stream of involution, and in that sense it is the beneficient stream that waters and maintains. On the other hand, if we look at our own destiny as being to return to the Source, then we have to go against the stream. Gurdjieff leaves you to see for yourself and many people so miss the point that they think he is being atheistic. Similarly with the phrase of materialism. What is not noticed is that materialism is not materialistic enough because it does not allow for more kinds of matter or higher energies. If we are speaking about constructing a cosmology which people are to believe in, then the question is whether we have to avoid offending people.

S: Is it useful to have a believable system before one understands what it is about in one's own experience?

JGB: It may not be a good service to people to make things plausible to them, because they will tend to accept without anything happening to them. It is not enough to say that experience is needed, it's a matter of what experience does for you. What does it do?

S: It enables you to see.

JGB: That is all that is necessary to say about it. Experience in itself is nothing, but experience gives you that possibility of seeing. If you see then you do not need somebody else to tell you. It's not always necessary to have external experiences; sometimes it is possible to see simply by what happens in your mind.

As time has gone on, it has become necessary for people to see more for themselves. In the process of growing up, the child has to be shown and then he learns how to see some things for himself and so it goes on. It has been so with mankind. At first people could see very little for themselves and they were very dependent on being told. Now we have to see more for ourselves.

When we are dealing with children we should put them in front of situations that make it possible for them to see. For example, it is more valuable for a child to see the result of selfish or self-indulgent actions for himself than to be told about them. Perhaps mankind is now going through a lesson of great importance in which he will be brought to see that his power over the material world does not give him any priviliges. To learn that lesson is essential. It will not come by being told, it will come by people seeing.

Notes From Meetings

DEATH: We have our body which dies and our personality with its feelings and thoughts which also dies in the second death. We have a third part—will—which does not die. Our will has us; we do not have it. Everybody has will. As long as we do not identify with the personality we can face death.

When there is no contact with the body, the person does not even know that he has died. Then there is the dissolution of the personality. But before that there is still an opportunity, even after the first death, of purifying the will if the work has not been done in life.

WILL: There are three parts to will—an individual, universal and absolute. The whole thing that J.G.B. is going after, what he repeatedly attempts to bring the students to see, is that there is a supernatural action beyond our minds which can work. No one comes anywhere near to seeing this.

People who do not have the "possibility of understanding" have a place, too. But their place is paradise; a dream. If we are really able to persist in saying "not this, not that," then we can become free.

We have been transferring the results of the meditation to P. She reported that she felt "electrical charges" shooting through her last night. J.G.B. said that we had really turned it on. This operates in the *alam-i arvah*, the middle world. Will is beyond that; will is completely unconditioned. When we do exercises that do not seem to be working, go on doing them and light will come.

SACRED IMPULSES: In a Gurdjieff lecture, the higher emotional and higher intellectual centres were discontinuous
stages. Our emotional nature has been dispersed. Naqshbandi
Sufis describe an exercise for unifying our emotional nature,
thus enabling direct perception. The whole of this nature is in
the region between our two breasts and between our throat and
middle part of the triangle between our breasts and solar
plexus. The sacred impulses are usually described as faith,
hope, and love, but there is one greater than these—the *wish* to
rejoin with the Source. The feeling of wish is followed by the
hope, here and now, to have the possiblitiy of return. "Belief" is
faith in our capacity to be acted on by the work; which is followed by conscience and obedience to our destiny. I obey the voice
of my conscience as I have faith in my potential for "going
beyond God." The impulse of love is for the Source.

The Naqshbandis refer to *latifas* or sensitive nodes in the region
of our breasts as the seat of these positive emotions. They must
be opened; awakened by the powers in the air.*

TO FREE ONESELF FROM SUFFERING: The technique requires one breath, but it takes practice. Nine times out of ten it is
possible to excrete the poisons of something which is injuring
our vanity, self-love, etc., by having the intention that the healing powers (from the Sun) in the second being food (Air) remove
the feeling state from us and enable a reversal to a deeper and
more essential part of our nature. One time out of ten our selves
will be really sensitive to something like possessiveness and the
suffering will be in a spot too deep for breath to remove.

THE FEELING OF EMPTINESS: The season of our states:
we must never let even our darkest despair influence anyone
else. We should just go on with our duty and separate from our
feelings of helplessness, etc. Negative states—*solioonen-
sius***—hits different types in different ways. We have to

---

*The first Sufi writer to refer to the *latifas* was the Kubrawi Shaikh Ala al–Daula
Samnani (d. 1335). At the Mongol court of Arghun he was in contact with Buddhist *bikkhus*, one of whom gave him great technical assistance in his spiritual
life. (The Cambridge History of Iran. Vol.5 pp. 536-7)

**This is a term coined by Gurdjieff to refer to times of "planetary tension" which
produces disturbances in the human psyche. In the mass, this tends to result in
wars and conflicts and the general increase of mass psychosis. But individuals
can receive energy for their struggle for inner freedom.

recognise it and "not carry anything that will break." States are like night and day—we cannot expect after a light sunny day that the next one will be sunnier. There is nothing accumulated in the world of states. It is only our experience which shows us about states and that is why it takes a long time. On the other hand we can penetrate to a further veil now in this moment.

I may pray, ask, etc., for this moment, to see all that I can see and hear—to see the void not only as the void but as the Source. If I am in a positive state, I sense the presence of the work, I wish to see all that can be seen, for this may be once in my life when the work is so present.

We are not free until we are free from everything.

GOING INTO THE FOREST: In the Hindu system there are four stages, beginning with the householder. These are not sequential but can be part of each day. We need not be sitting cross-legged to transform energies.

FEELING AND BEING: Awareness of feeling. Watch how much feeling there is of feeling. There can be this awareness and seeing that there is no "I."

In the exercise be aware of the whole. This state is not awareness of "I." We cannot be aware of it. "I" is our will —awareness is our being. It is neither "I" nor not "I." It is closer to say that we see we are empty rather than filled. We see that the sacred impulses are neither leaving nor entering us—they are the conditions. This is "I am."

The union of our self (being) and our own "I" (will) is in the impulses. They are from the one Source. They are only different impulses in ourselves.

CONTEMPLATION: This is the culmination of the "first line of work."* Whenever we see we have hurt someone or acted in a way with bad consequences, we should bring experiences of a similar kind in front of ourselves—not go right out and struggle. We can struggle with a new insight after we have contemplated. This is given in "Form and Sequence." (see *Beelzebub's Tales*). "Outer and Inner Worlds" (Third Series) is Gurdjieff on comtemplation.

---

*cf., *The Sevenfold Work*, J.G. Bennett, Coombe Springs Press, 1979.

HUMAN STUPIDITY: "I was going to do this, but I did that."
Two kinds of initiative—one in mind and one in feelings.
Change of usage of the word "I" in one sentence.

There is a tremendous gap between what we profess and what
we practice. We set ourselves to work and most of the time we
are in a stupor. There is a great compassion working. No limit to
human stupidity and no limit to the compassion of the Spirit.

We have to set ourselves not to take when something is
available. Remember Gurdjieff's decision not to use his powers.
The ability not to take is what will enable a core of people to be
prepared for the crisis. Struggle with this enables the formation
of the *kesdjan* body. It is this struggle that gives our higher body
form. If J.G.B. were asked the Beelzebub question about how to
save people on earth he would answer, "by allowing them to see
the state of their own souls."

THE PERFECTED MAN: In every breath he is being born
with the inhalation—becoming present—he is dying with ex-
halation—liberated. He is present in the world but free from it.

AFFIRMATION NEEDS A VEHICLE: The vehicle of the affirming force in man is vision. The higher centres do not make
our knowledge deeper, etc.,but create a union of knowing and
will. As it is, "we have no power to do what we see and no wish
to do what we can do."

REINCARNATION: We see that we have to suffer if we
throw away opportunities. It is not that the *work* dies if we blow
it. The point is that *we* have to pay—suffer—and thus we have
further lives to live.

THE WORK WORKS: If we say that in the work there is no
moral obligation, people tend to interpret this as saying that
anything is okay. The part in the Sermon on the Mount, "except
you exceed the pharisees etc.,"is not a moral thing. The whole
of the Sermon on the Mount cannot be understood unless seen
as not moral. It is beyond right and wrong.

Will creates feelings which simply need a channel, the rest goes
on. The point is that we must keep "alive" and then the Work
works. The obligation is to take care of our body and then the
rest will take place.

Almost to fail is to reach perfection—this is all that is needed.

WORSHIP: Worship needs to be done in a society. There are different forms of worship in the different religions. There is this problem. In Christianity the form of worship is reserved for the priest. The understanding of worship passed down from the apostles to the present day through the Christian chain of transmission. In the Jewish religion it is the same with the Rabbis. They were able to participate in a true form of worship.

The Islamic tradition is different. Here we have the *namaz* which is an authentic form of worship. The *namaz* is lead by the *imam* who needs no special initiation. The way of worshipping is each towards the same Source.

The different religions have all sprung from the same Source but they are limited. The Source has a channel through each religion and all are necessary. There are also threads connecting every one of us with the Source—we each have our own way.

Adam, Abraham, Moses and Jesus: all the prophets are Messengers and none are "better." The Islamic tradition had the role of reconciling the others. Muhammad preached "All religions are one; there is only one God." We see that this is the motto of the brotherhood Gurdjieff mentions in the last chapter of *Meetings with Remarkable Men.*

The *zikr* is a form of worship. There are free *zikrs* such as the *latihan*, and there are those which are affirming Allah. We are narrow and closed in. The *zikr* opens the heart.

BRINGING UP CHILDREN: All who have any dealings with children should be very much on their guard against suggesting likes and dislikes to children. Mr. Gurdjieff once said that if a parent sees someone suggesting likes and dislikes to children he has, "Right to kill. Stick knife in back."

THE INNER WORLD: It is inner, not somewhere else. There is not another world somewhere over there that is called the spiritual world, and a world here that is called the material world. But there is one thing; the inner world cannot be reached by the personality, for personality is alien to it. This is very hard to accept. It is very hard for us to picture what we would be like without our personality. What remains if it is taken away?

SPIRIT. PERSONALITY IS NOT 'I', PERSONALITY
IS AN ACCIDENTAL ACCUMULATION OF REFUSE
IN & OF MATERIAL WORLD.
                                    FROM
                                EXPERIENCES
                                    -'G'

Part VI

When set in the six dimensional framework, the future can be seen as existing though not actual. It exists in potential form and has its own pattern and structure. This accounts for the influence of the future, even when not foreseen or foreseeable, upon present events. It also allows for the seemingly incompatible phenomena of:

a) CAUSALITY. Past causes future. Future predictable.
b) CONTINGENCY. Future unpredictable. Uncertainty.
c) FINALITY. Future influences past. Goal-seeking purposive activity.
d) FATE. Future predetermined by its own pattern, but only in limited cases, e.g. fate of individual or group. Astrology.
e) FREE WILL. Future undetermined. Spontaneous action possible. Causa sui.
f) DESTINY. The concept of personal destiny that is not predetermined or compulsive, but realised through acts of free choice. Dharma. Predestination.
g) PROVIDENCE. Guidance of history by Divine, or at least a power higher than man.
h) THE UNIVERSE as continuous creation.

The general inadequacy of both traditional and modern views points to the need for a new theory, especially as the future presents itself today as more threatening and unpredictable than it appeared 70 years ago when Einstein's relativity first disturbed the classical belief in absolute space and time.

(From a synopsis of a projected book: What Makes The Future?)

The Existence of the Future

I want to talk about knowing the future. Can we know what does not exist and does this mean that in some way the future exists? First of all, we have to understand that the present does not exist in a particularly convincing way. We are always concerned with seeing what has just happened, not what is happening. We are aware of traces of past events, never of the present. The carpet I look at is the trace of light signals originating in the past. If then we say that the present does not exist, and also we say that the future which has not happened does not exist, then existence starts looking very thin. It is better to say the whole lot exists, in some way or other. After all, the world is pretty solid, and experience is rich and varied and it cannot all amount to nothing.

We know the past from the traces left behind and we know the future in terms of expectations and calculations. There are certain things, like the Sun rising tomorrow, that only a cosmic catastrophe can prevent. Such things surely must exist.

I have just put the porridge into the oven for tomorrow's breakfast. I am confident that the combination of ingredients and the heat of the oven will form porridge by the morning. The arrangement or construction of things has an influence on the future. There is a certain arrangement of people and furniture in the room during this lecture. When I decided to give the lecture, this arrangement was not present. I wanted to sort out certain ideas and thought that what would come out would be of interest to me and to you.

The making of porridge and the giving of a lecture are examples of looking to the future as the end of a process. In the course of the process certain combinations have to come about. These are put together because there is some picture of the end result. We have something here that is the opposite of causality because we are operating in the present in terms of the future; whereas in causality, the future is the outcome of what there is in the present.

There are many events that we cannot influence, no matter how much we concentrate our thoughts, such as the time of the rising of the Sun or where it will rise. Such events are fully determined and subject to causality. But the future is not all of a kind. Only some events are fully determined whereas others are only partially so. Uncertainty increases in a very rapid way with the number of interactions we have to take into account. There is a vastly greater number of relationships than objects related, and an even greater number of orders or arrangements of relationships.* This explains the possibility of contingent events.

In the world of living things, we cannot make sense of events without accepting that processes are future-oriented, directed towards some goal. This does not mean that living cells go around thinking about the future as we do. Goal-seeking is a certain relationship with the future that does not have to be mental. It is certainly not a form of causality, or of being determined by the past. The living entity feeds, reproduces, grows towards various end points. There are constructive processes that produce concentrations of order. What we call the genetic pattern does not *determine* the future. For the acorn to grow into an oak certain environmental influences must be present. The acorn has *potential;* which I am saying is a real kind of existence, so that even if it fails to germinate, or is eaten by an animal or crowded out by other trees, that potential *still exists.*

The idea that potential exists should not be strange since physics depends a great deal on the concept of unobservable potential energy that can be converted into some observable motion or activity. "Where" this potential exists occupied me for a long time. I am now saying that its locus is *in the future* where there is ample room for it. When the acorn fails to grow into an oak tree, this potential will be used up in some other way.

*This idea is developed in the first chapter of J.G. Bennett's book *Creation,* Dramatic Universe Study Series 3. Coombe Springs Press 1978. It is based on Georg Cantor's transfinite numbers.

Such a way of talking about this is not usual. It is very difficult to think about time at all without turning it into some kind of space. Time is quite unlike space. We must remember that when people think about things existing, they are picturing them within some imaginary present moment in which nothing is really happening. Once we grasp that time really is a condition of existence then these ideas about the future begin to come quite easily.

So far we have talked about the determined and semi-determined future and about the potential future. Now we must look at what is called *fate*. This can be known. There is too much evidence about the effectiveness of astrology to ignore. It can be used to predict a great deal about a life. Astrology is built on knowledge of the place and time of birth and probably of conception. It took me a long time to accept the fact of astrology for, on the face of it, it is absurd that knowledge of the position of the planets at a particular time could lead to any real insight into an individual human life.

The pattern of fate is neither causal nor future oriented. It accompanies a life throughout as if it were the warp on which the life is woven. It does not compel, but enters into everything that happens. And such patterns apply not only to individual people, but to groups, institutions, and maybe to the whole historical process. We speak of the fate of nations, of the ill-fated city, and Gurdjieff even used the phrase "ill-fated planet" of our own earth. There are also such things as favourable and unfavourable days which are the subject matter of divination. It is possible to discern a pattern of events in very strange ways, such as throwing yarrow stalks when using the *I Ching*. In times past, people used the flight of birds, or the entrails of sacrificial animals and today people use tea leaves. Common to all these ways is the use of some arbitrarily produced pattern, and the principle must be that all patterns produced without constraint within a region of experience are related. A large scale pattern will tend to reproduce itself on a small scale and will then look like an organising influence.

Fate is a pattern which exists in the future zone. It is somehow able to make certain events more probable than others. This gives human life a shape it would not have otherwise. We say that as complexity increases, so does uncertainty and unpredictability. Yet as we move more and more in that direction, as we do when considering the lives of people, we find regularity again. We might expect human life to be much more unpredictable than it is because so many factors are influencing it.

Now we have three future zones. First, that which is going to be the outcome of past events. Second, that which is potential, like the oak tree in the seed (perhaps we should say that the tree is in the time of the seed, in its future time). Third, the patterns which give shape to complex events, which are not end points but "characters." In none of these is there any need to talk about freedom. They are not regions of spontaneity.

I want to introduce another idea, that of *destiny,* as a counterpart to fate. Destiny is the possibility of creation that we have and it is in this creation that we have our essential freedom. In one way, it can be called the freedom to be ourselves that Goethe spoke about, "The striving to become what one already is." To be what we are, we have to find our way through all the influences of future events, of our genetic pattern, and our fate. Destiny is our *dharma,* the part we have to play in the cosmic drama. It is a role we have to create and it is not determined for us.

There is a destiny not only for us as individuals but also for the human race as a whole, and our private destiny must in some way be an element in the greater whole.

We can put it to ourselves that there are patterns which constrain and patterns which invite and open and are totally permissive. There is nothing in this world that compels us to fulfill our destiny and when we understand that, we can understand what freedom is. If we fulfill our destiny, we have our eternal place. If not, we fall out of that place. Maybe this is allowed for as Nature allows for the many acorns which fail to become oak trees and turns them into use, decay being as important as growth in the living world.

Fate is with us all the time and presses in on us. But because it is not causal, there is always the possiblility of finding our way round it by means of the immense uncertainty there is in the world. It is very probable that we have more than a single fate and that our lives can change their course. In Ouspensky's theory of recurrence much is made of this, but it does not radically affect the principle that the fulfillment of our destiny may always have to be done through overcoming our fate.

I will finish with a story. A certain king heard of Moses and his achievements and commissioned a portrait to be made of him so that he could see what sort of man the prophet was. When the painting was brought to him, he summoned his astrologers and wise men to give pronouncement. To his surprise, they said such things as, "He is a man eaten up with pride. He is filled with anger. He is a supreme egoist." The king's bewilderment was answered by one wise man who got up and said, "Yes, such is the character of Moses, but he has overcome his nature and that is why he is creating the destiny for an entire group of people."

Vorstellung

JGB: The German word *vorstellung* is usually translated simply as "representation," but I think it is the best word to designate what enables "will" to enter this world. There is an action in which we place before ourselves what we are "willing"- this is the *vorstellung.* By representing an event to ourselves, we can create the means by which the event can come about. We are part of the event itself and this is not really mysterious. It is a creative action that is particularly important at this moment of history when we have to *create*, not make, a new world. Some people say this is to be done by thinking the new world, but thinking has to be understood in a much stronger way than in the ordinary sense.

When I use the word *vorstellung* I do not mean thinking, but something very strong and direct. The act of representation is not to put the image outside of ourselves, but inside ourselves, so that we really experience it. It is very important to train this power of representation. Working at it together can be a great help, because by oneself it takes much time and determination. That is why I want us to organize our activities for a time without any formal plan, relying entirely on the *vorstellung* we will make every morning.

S: Is the making of thought forms concerning our childrens' future a good thing?

JGB: If you dare to think you know what is truly desirable! The whole quesion of how we can influence the future is one I want to take up again later on.

S: A few days ago you and someone else spoke about being sensitive to this house as more than a material object. Yesterday I was doing the *zikr* in front of the house and suddenly it seemed like a living being and that night I saw it like that again, the house and this place as a whole.

JGB: It is very difficult to avoid using the word "life" in talking about this kind of thing. Life is one form in which the world is realising itself. Life is life. But we have this picture of material things as inert unless *we* project meaning into them, which is a mistake. You saw correctly. The house has a certain presence of its own to which we should be sensitive. Patterns of energies become associated with material objects and some people have by nature the power to be aware of them. This is called *psychometry.* They can take an object in their hands and tell many things that have happened to it simply by putting themselves in tune with the energy pattern. The patterns can be harmful, beneficient or neutral, coherent or chaotic. This kind of perception is to be encouraged but it comes naturally through the exercises we have been doing. It comes with the development of the inner *kesdjan* body of man. But if it is artificially forced, the formation of the inner body can be disturbed. Many mistakes can happen through people doing this. I remember a man who discovered he had amazing powers of dowsing. This was in the Indian army. It led him into healing, but when I met him by chance in England, he was near to destroying himself. It often happens that people who overuse psychic power without having developed the strength of the *kesdjan* body have something drained away and the physical body is left defenceless. Tuberculosis is then a common thing. It is really very important to know that one should never use special powers unless one has very good guidance and has become very strong.

S: I'm gaining confidence that as far as planning goes, the only thing I can do is to try to feel what is right to do the next moment. I can't worry about next year. But it's not the same as being unable to commit myself to something because one day I will like it and the next day I'm bummed out and not interested. I was also thinking that if different people in the group feel different things, it will no longer be appropriate for the group to be together, or it will change by itself. If we are proceeding step by step we do not need to worry about these things.

JGB: Not only don't need to, but it would be quite contrary to what we are trying to do. And I want to say this. You used the word "plan." In the ordinary meaning of the word, a plan is a wicked destructive thing which must never be thought of. If you make a plan, you condemn yourself to live in a hell. The world in which you can predict the future, where you prepare things in this way, is hell. It is the material world from which we want to escape. Everyone can see how planning creates hell, on a small or large scale. Now, how is it possible to reconcile this realisation that planning is a hell-making thing with what I propose of making a representation of something that is to come in the future?

In my own language, "plan" is connected with time and *vorstellung* with *hyparxis.* * I have spoken before about expectation where what we expect does not happen. If we make an expectation into a constraint, as we do with a plan, then either we make ourselves mechanical, surrendering all initiative, or make ourselves suffer all the unforeseeable consequences. That is why it is hell.

In the way of *vorstellung* we do not make a plan—we open up certain possibilities for something to happen. We can look at the situation in front of us and say, "Is this setting me free, or making me a slave?" Plans always fail because if the projected result is achieved, the price is not what one expected. If one is not prepared to pay the price, the result will not come. Only the behavior of a machine can be planned.

We need to train ourselves to have strong mental images or thought forms. There is a substance for this, but for the most part it is misused. It cannot be inactive because its very nature is that it must act. Therefore if we have no command for it, it acts by itself and produces in us streams of association, day dreams and fantasies. It is not necessary that we should control this and command it at all times. It is necessary on the contrary, that we should spend a certain amount of our day without attempting to concentrate this energy but allowing it to flow freely. But we get into the way of not using it at all and because of this we have far less command over our lives than we are entitled to and obliged to have. We should have control over our own lives and not be dependent on other people. Only a few people have the necessary strength of mind to do this. The majority

*This is a key concept in *The Dramatic Universe*. Also, *cf., Existence*, Dramatic Universe Study Series 2. *Hyparxis* is the dimension associated with hazard, decision, and the direction or kind of time in which something can realise itself.

allow themselves either to drift or to be dominated by their egoistic impulses. They do things—but only in order to satisfy themselves. This is just as much slavery as doing things by dependence on other people. It is necessary to be in such a balance that "non-desires predominate over desires."* You must realise that we have this creative power. Everyone of us has it. If the thought form is strong enough, it creates the event.

(A question was asked about the use of thought forms to help to accomplish a task.)

JGB: You must understand this; that we create a thought form but it must have a life of its own. It must not be something fixed or crystallized in the sense of being rigid.

When it comes to working on some feature of yourself, you have to learn about certain things. You have to learn how to have a picture of the positive state that you want to achieve in such a way that it does not attach itself to your egoism and self-love (or the satisfaction of having achieved getting rid of such a weakness and so on) otherwise you end up really worse off than before.

---

*From Gurdjieff's *Beelzebub's Tales to His Grandson.*

Outstripping Time
(November 1967)

I have been told that I am in search of absolute knowledge. What I have been in search of, really, is a way of looking at the world and at life that would make sense to me without sweeping the awkward bits under the carpet. There are plenty of ways of making sense of a good deal of the world and of a good deal of our experience, but when it comes to making sense of everything without compromising over the awkward and difficult bits, then it is a search which will probably go on as long as the universe exists and certainly as long as man lives here on earth.

Various principles that seem true and inevitably right to us conflict with one another in such a way that it seems we are forced to make a choice. Then, sometime or other, people come and say that they have seen something beyond these principles, each of which had seemed to be final and absolute. We had certain notions about time which were held until this century and then they began to be less definite and unmistakable than before. Old certainties dissolve and hopes are formed of a new certainty.

I want to suggest ways of looking at our situation in time—but with no wish to annihilate time. What time brings into our experience is an enrichment as well as a danger. Sometimes people think that they want to open their minds to a timeless reality in which there will be no change, no death or decay. They believe that that is what they are searching for. But if they look at it squarely, no matter how perfect the changeless state might be, there would still be something in them that would deeply revolt against it. And yet, it is true that the "perpetual perishing" of our experience is also something that we are not able to accept. What we are really after is something intermediate between the perishing of the moment and a static unchanging state.

The unchanging state is really one without any experience in it. It is a psychological fact that what we experience is change, not the unchanging. If any part of our experience ceases to change, it disappears from our consciousness. When experiments have been done with people placed in a totally neutral unchanging environment, it has been found that they lose consciousness of their surroundings and eventually suffer intense hallucinations. Even without psychological explanations we should all of us know quite deeply that without change, one part of our reality which is essential for us would go. Therefore, we cannot seriously hope for the annihilation of time, not at any rate as far as consciousness is concerned.

A potential for experience can be preseved in a timeless state. For example, in the farming industry the technique of artificial insemination has been introduced in which the male sperm is frozen at the temperature of liquid nitrogen. As far as one can see, the potential of the sperm is preserved without loss and it can be maintained in that state for years and still produce satisfactory offspring. There is no reason to suppose that the same experiment could not be made with mankind. A man living today could fertilize a woman living a thousand years hence and produce normal and healthy offspring.

It is also, of course, possible for us to have our experiences stored in much the same kind of way in certain kinds of memories, which seem to go into cold storage and can be awakened after many years, even over the whole span of a life, so that the experience renews itself as if there had been no intervening interval of time. I expect most of us have memories of this kind which are different from memories about what has happened, or knowledge of what has happened. They are timelessly preserved experiences. Our ordinary memories that we can recall or think about undoubtedly change. Anyone who has kept a diary which goes back a good long time is always astonished at how what appears to be an accurate memory of a certain event has actually transformed in the course of time.

Perhaps one has thought about it, or talked about it and so on. Even memory is not timeless if it enters into experience. It is only timeless if it is able to go out of experience into some region of preservation.

I do think that there is such a region of preservation of experience. I call it *eternity* and I think that it is as much a part of the real world as the events which go on in time. We see it in the example of the frozen sperm, or in a storage battery, or in the atom which can preserve its potential for transformation for millions of years. The conservation of potentiality is a well-established property in both the material and the living world. Psychologically, it also seems well established and I think it is very probable that some kind of conservation similar to that of "imperishable memories" goes beyond the death of the physical body. I remember a very powerful experience I had about the conservation of the potentialities of young men who were at school with me and who were killed in the 1914-1918 war. Though I was deeply wounded by the loss of these lives, I became directly aware that their potentialities were completely preserved and able to germinate afresh in some way or other. This is an incommunicable experience and of course unverifiable with our present means, but it admitted of no doubt in me.

I want to emphasize that this preservaton is not the same as the annihilation of time. It merely means going out of time and being able to re-enter it. That this is possible seems obvious to me, though it might appear very strange to most people and just an exagerated way of expressing the fact that potential is conserved. To me, it is not only obvious but very significant: potentialities are taken out of time, put in cold storage and are able to re-appear in another time and also, naturally, in another place.

Time is a separation in the field of potentiality—it separates what will be from what might be. If I toss a coin and obtain a head, then the tail is a "might-have-been;" but this tail that "might" have turned up and did not is just as much a part of the real situation as the head that did turn up.* The unrealised potentialities are not nothing, but they are not actual. If this is

---

*For a more detailed discussion of this difficult point, *cf., Hazard,* J.G. Bennett, Coombe Springs Press, 1976.

right, the actual world is not the whole world and time is that part of the world which has been, is, or will be actual.

In this "becoming actual" there is a gradation. Some things become actual completely and without blurring—like the head in the case of tossing a coin. This is characteristic of material events, where there is a sharp distinction between actual and potential. We are able to discover laws concerning the way things become actual, and this enables us to make predictions. This predictableness of the actualization is the characteristic of time that somehow touches us on the raw. This is especially so for death, even though it is not predicatble in the way in which an eclipse is. Death is simply a very probable event. It is a consequence of the second law of thermodynamics which asserts the low probability of maintaining a high order such as that of our bodies. Life processes do not actualise with the same sharpness as physical events.

Beside the prediction of material events and the probabilities of life events, we have contact with actualization through premonition. Precognition is always about some physical event, but it impinges on human experience. A famous example is that of the many premonitions people had of the sinking of the Lusitania. Such events are determined, but they involve such complexities that calculation, even that of some supposed super computer in the brain cannot explain how this knowledge is gained. How would the computer programme come to be written?

I want to draw attention to the point that if contact with a future event is possible, then the future event is *there.* Are we then to conclude that nothing can be done about it? Is all that is going to happen frozen into a four-dimensional matrix of space and time? It was this picture, which I came across in Minkowski's paper, that caused me tremendous emotional upheaval. I read about it in 1916 and it seemed to me that the argument—that we live in an absolute world in which events are arbitrarily carved as between time and space and according to the way the observer happens to be moving—was complete and unanswerable. How then could I view myself as a being able to influence future events? About 1920 I came to the clear conclusion that this dilemna could only be resolved by postulating an additional dimension, the one that I called "eternity." For a long time I was satisfied with this solution and it was not until many years later that I saw that even this was not enough—one still had to account for the possibility of moving between the world of potential and the world of actualisation.*

There is the connection with future events that we call precognition and there is also postcognition, that is, a connection with past events that does not depend upon memory, nor upon a reconstruction. The question is whether these contacts with past and future events can serve any useful purpose. I think it was Priestley, in his book on time, who introduced the concept of F.I.P. (future-influencing-present, or future-influencing-past) He gave examples from his own life of having done certain things which made no sense at the time, but later were seen to be preparation for something which he did not know was to occur. I have seen the same thing in my own life. It has no evidential value for another person. Nevertheless, it is one of the most significant phenomena in human life.

If we only knew the inevitable consequences of our actions, many things that we do would have to be different. But there is a veil that prevents us from seeing, and so we go on producing causes of suffering and disaster for ourselves and for others. We say that if there were precognition, it would make an enormous difference to our lives. But this is true only for cognition which is of *the future which can be changed*—to have foreknowledge of events which are already determined will not help us.

We know that the Sun will rise tomorrow and we arrange our lives accordingly, but there is nothing we can do about it. But if I had foreknowledge that tomorrow I would run over somebody in a car, I would stay at home. That is what I believe, but if the accident were a material reality that *had* to happen, then I would be unable to do anything but go out in the car and run the person over, no matter how much I knew about it. Such things have been reported—the terrifying fatal awareness of something that is going to happen from which there is no escape.

We have to ask ourselves whether there is some kind of knowledge about the future which is useful, because there is something we can do about it. If we are to think in this way, then we have to think that there is more than one future. For me, this

---

*This is the dimension of *hyparxis*.

is an undoubted truth. The future is a spectrum of events ranging from the wholly determined to the wholly undetermined. It is a matter of free decision for those who are able to exist in that rarified atmosphere where nothing is determined from the past. This all follows from what I have said about potentiality. Free decision is possible if one is able to chase potential into the realm of preservation and enable it to become actual without concerning oneself with actualisation on the pre-determined level.

The idea of being able to travel out of space and time into another region is not so fanciful. We do this whenever we make a free choice, which is possible only when we are confronted with more than one possible event in a given situation. When we make this choice—and it is always a hard choice—it involves some sacrifice of the actual in order to gain the potential. When we make it, we go out of the determinate world into a different region. But then all that we ever do is to make a kind of loop in the line of time, because we are so constructed that we are not able to maintain ourselves for very long on a potential higher than that of our own bodies. Therefore we find ourselves constantly back in the material world.

In dreams we find ourselves under conditions that are totally extraordinary and we are able to move with greater freedom. But this all falls short of what I mean by "outstripping time." I will give a physical picture. Imagine that I am in contact with an astronomer on the star Sirius. Now, light takes eight and a half years to travel between the Sun and Sirius and to receive a message from him and for him to receive a reply would take seventeen years. If I have telepathic powers, I could tell him to alter his signal without taking eight and a half years to do so; but to tell him to alter his signal, so that the message *in the light reaching me now* changes, would require me to reach him eight and a half years *in the past,* when the signal started on its journey. It would be a communication from the future to the past which changes what happens. Then we can imagine the Sirian astronomer joining us, when he himself would be sending messages back to himself.

I believe that in man there is one part that is capable of this extraordinary journey. In the physical example, I talked about sending of light signals to establish a background of ordinary time. But there is no physical mechanism by which one can transport oneself ahead of time. People talk about the powers of thought or consciousness, but it is hard to say what they can or cannot do. There is something less material and less conditioned than either of these, even a timeless consciousness. That is *will*.

Our will is a strange thing. It is ourselves; it is "I myself." "I am," as Schopenhauer said, "my will." Yet, when I ask myself about this will in my life, can I ever say that I am making an act of will—or is it simply the transformation of the different substances of which I am made—body, thoughts, feelings, consciousness and so on? I am always brought to the brink of what I cannot understand. There is something which is unable to take the plunge and to shed anything that would condition my will. The will does not have to be conditioned. It is only conditioned because in order to act it needs instruments. If my will works through my body, it is conditioned by the laws which govern my body. That is why it is so difficult to find any convincing evidence that there is such a thing as free will at all. When we begin to penetrate into our inner states of consciousness, there does seem to be something that is more free, but it is still conditioned. But we can suppose that as we go more deeply we come to a region in which the will is without limit and nothing is determined. That region becomes the future for everything else since nothing has happened there. I call this region the *hyparchic future* because I use the word *hyparxis* to mean that which enables us to move across the streams of time and space and even of eternity. It is the inherent freedom that is associated with our will.

I believe that this region of the *hyparchic future* is responsible for the phenomena of the future influencing the past. In some way, our will can outstrip time and we can make decisions before the events in which the decisions become conscious and tangible.

I think that this notion of outstripping time accounts for some of the deepest intuitions of mankind, such as the notion attributed to Gautama Buddha of the state of *Nirvana*. This is a state of non-existence but not of nothingness; a state in which there is neither being nor time; but also a state that is incomparably rich. This notion has always been extremely perplexing to people because it seemed that it required non-existence and yet was asserted to be the state of perfection of being. In my opinion, there is nothing very difficult about it, once one has become accustomed to the kind of multi-dimensional world I have been talking about, and also when one associates the nirvanic state with the will rather than the being of man. The will is able to produce its own form, although in itself it is formless.

I think that there is no contradiction between the Buddhist and the Christian doctrine. The latter has been miserably and wretchedly misinterpreted as a kind of time state in the future. But what is said clearly in the Gospels shows that it is referring to this other kind of future, not the future of the material world. It is a future which is free from time yet not less than time. The extraordinary saying, "I go to prepare a place for you," has always struck me as being one of the most remarkable utterances conceivable. It amounts to the assertion, "I am going ahead in time in order to prepare something which has not yet happened." I have never found anybody who has seen the extraordinary significance of an assertion of this kind—that it is possible to go ahead of time and act before events.

It has taken me all of fifty years to clarify this for myself. I started thinking about these things in 1917 and I have had exceptional opportunities, for I met people who furnished experiences that were material for understanding. I know that your chief obstacle in understanding will be thinking that it is very easy, that it is some kind of precognition. Precognition of the determined future is no more remarkable than telepathy in the present. Whereas going ahead of time means going ahead of where there is anything at all.

Mental Images

We have learned something about transferring a mental image from the thinking to the moving center. We have made experiments with concerted mental images of events, and seen how these images exert an organising influence in their constituents. We know that it is possible to have some power over material events, even when they are not under our immediate control. But mental images play a part in our lives in many other ways. The power of imagination—the making of mental images—is part of our equipment as human beings. Gurdjieff ascribes this power to a certain energy which he calls *piandjoehary*, and says that it can make or destroy, one can lose oneself or find oneself. How strange it is that one of the highest powers with which man is endowed can destroy everything in him and make him useless.

I want you to see what happens when mental images become relevant to what is happening in us, when there is an entry of the mental image into the actual world. It is of some importance when we can see the transition from the state in which imagination and behaviour are divorced from each other— so that we are living two kinds of life, one of fantasy and one of activity—to the state in which they work together.

I am sitting here and looking ahead to what I have to do next. I have to get some information by making a telephone call to America. I see how I am going to do it. Having formed a mental image in this way, I shall do something about it within the next hour. If I fail to do this, then it will be because I will be engaged in some fantasy that will drive it out of my mind. If I do it, it will be because the mental image and the behaviour fit together and then it will be easy and I will not waste any time. When it is rightly prepared, I need not concern myself with it and I am able to occupy myself with other duties.

In every task there is a structure, but in order for it to become alive it has to be energised. When you really take on a responsibility a mental image is formed, and you should know that this image has to be made substantial enough to have an effect on you.

S: I want to ask about mental images that form themselves. I went to the schedule and saw that I had an exeat (free day). Immediately a mental image came to me about what I would do on that day. This seems quite different from making a mental image intentionally.

JGB: The mental image can form itself spontaneously, and indeed, there is always something spontaneous, because there must be some starting point. But what is it that makes the image effectual? In the example that you gave, you can say yes or no to the image that comes. You can reject it and set yourself to do something quite different. It is important to treat the mental image as something in its own right and therefore worthy of respect. If you let it all drift, you may do what you pictured in your mind and be satisfied, or wish that you had not done it, but nothing significant will have happened. Mental images have a hold of their own on reality; they are not just states in us. There are many species of mental image. There are the "building castles in Spain" kind, where one is neither in Spain nor can one afford to build castles. There are spontaneous images which are the opening of possibilities. There are mental images which are formed by reiteration so that the picture is always there, representing something that is said over and over again. There are the kind which are created by us in order to bring about some action. There are creative images which have the character of uniqueness. I am simply speaking to you at random.

S: There is something to do with visualisation that comes into my working with the compost, trying to find out if it is right.

JGB: Properly speaking, what tells us about compost is more our hands than our eyes. (It seems to me that our compost is never allowed to settle for long enough.) Somehow or other we have to feel for it. It is partly a matter of looking and partly a matter of touching, but that is not all. How is it for you? When you talk about having a picture of the compost, is it just that you see a mass of it or have you felt a different contact with it?

S: It has been a whole process. I started looking at what has been happening in our compost and felt it did not look right. I decided to get involved with it and read a lot about what was supposed to happen and what goes on inside it. The picture I got from the information merged with the actual working with the materials and now it is still a continuous process of touch and feel and see.

JGB: (After much discussion of over-hastiness in using the compost), In this case, visualisation means to be in actual contact. It is not simply seeing something from the outside. Anyone can picture a heap with organic material being dumped onto it, and they can picture the look of it at different stages; but visualisation means more than that.

S: When we were working on the wall, the day we were using a mental image that we created together, I was stuck with a very restricted bit of wall. But in one of the pauses I became aware of the whole event and even where the work had gotten to in the different places. At least, in my mind's eye. A similar thing happened the other day when I had many things to do, but by keeping it open, the day gradually formed itself and things came into my mind which were part of that day. It was all quite easy and straight-forward.

JGB: That is where the mental image begins to take over from simple visualisation. There are gradations in this. Sometimes when one makes a mental image with what one knows, one finds it in things that one does not know, as if it is putting one in touch with something beside what one put into it.

S: During the day, I would sometimes come to do something that I could recognise from the visualisation, but it would be in a slightly different form. It is a bit vague.

JGB: It is a very important observation which we must speak about. The creation of a mental image does not destroy freedom. It is not like a plan, where one is imposing something on the future or when something unexpected happens and one has to force things to make them keep to the plan. Usually when one forces things, the game is not worth the candle. One may achieve the result but lose too much in the process; or have it changed into something else that one pretends to be what one intended. When, on the contrary, there is a real visualisation, something will happen that is in accordance with the *dharma*, the inherent pattern of the situation. The mental image has the power to produce an event in which all the uncertainties are assimilated. It has the power to evolve, and it is then that we come across something unexpected in what we ourselves have visualised.

S: I have two observations that illustrate some of the difficulties. In the first I made a mental image of getting together with J. The image was discrete and I was sure that it would be effectual after I had let it go. And things did work out in the right way. In the second, I was working on making a bench in the sauna. After two-and-a-half hours I saw that what had actually happened was very different from the mental image I thought I had formed. What you said about the different kind of contact with the compost example really came home.

JGB: We have to learn how to form mental images from within. It is connected with what I said yesterday about different levels in life. If we are seeing something with our eyes we are seeing it from the outside, in the world of bodies; but if we want to see how it is working itself out, we must try not to see it as if it were something on a cinema screen, in succession, but somehow get the feel of it. Then the contact is of a different kind and it is effectual.

S: I seem to spend most of my day in pure fantasy. The idea of making a mental image really irritates me. When we stop on the hour, I find that I can't remember what I was doing in the hour that is gone and it freaks me out to look ahead to what is going to happen in the next hour. Yet I do things. I was planting out flowers and was determined to get them all in. But I missed one. Yesterday I was ill but had to go back and plant the remaining flower. There seems to be no connection between what I want to do and what I do.

JGB: You are in the awkward position that is called "sitting between two stools." In dealing with this world, you either have to get at it from the outside—bodies dealing with bodies—or through this other way of the mental image, but you have no control over it. (He goes on to give specific personal advice.)

S: Two things. One was about visualising a physical activity. There was hardly any picture at all, it was just like a point
in a line. I had to shift a large stone block and had not much idea
of how to do it. Getting it out was in my mind's eye and it happened. I find that in physical activities the mental image is connected with the determination to do it and there is nothing like a
picture involved. Everything went very exactly.

JGB: Let us take that for the moment. With practice, it is
true that it ceases to be necessary to spend much time, or even
any time at all, with making the mental image. That is because
the moving center is very fast. When it is something it knows
about, you have only to say, "Do this," and you know that it
will. You have only to say, "I'll go for a mile walk," and you
immediately know that the walk will be done even if it is very
awkward and inconvenient. Once your moving center can
understand your language, it quickly grasps what to do. If you
have the connection there is no need to think about it. Making
the connection does take time and practice.

S: The second thing is about the arising of thought forms
which appear to have some effect on the actual course of events.
Continuing my first example, a picture came into my mind of
the stone beng removed from the site, using a vehicle; and
everything for this came into phase yesterday, the people, the
vehicle, and the opportunity.

Then today it came into my mind to recognise the unusual pattern in various places. I saw myself saying, I'll take a shovel and
fill up the hole where the stone was." Then I thought to myself,
"There is no time, I have house duties, I have already decided
what to do with my lunch hour." Then it came to me, "Well, the
tools are quite the opposite end of the garden. Wouldn't it be
nice if I had a spade here at hand." Then it passed from my
mind. In the afternoon I went to the sauna where I was allocated
work. No one else was there. Then, without thinking about it,
there was a shovel lying against the wall and I thought I would
go and fill up the hole. It was strange, the shovel being there and
I had not expected it to be, and the gap of time which I had not
expected either. I am curious about how things work like that
because it has happened before in my life and sometimes about
things that I did not want to happen.

JGB: If the future were fully determined then it would be possible to know in advance that the shovel would be there. You might have a sixth sense about it, because the number of uncertainties is so large that it would be impossible to calculate it according to causal principles. But what happens is that our own state is a factor in the course of events. Saying this at first seems to be a bit like saying we can take a train to London or to Edinburgh and which we take depends upon our mood; but it is more than that. If we are in a London mood then there *are no trains* to Edinburgh. This, which at first must seem absurd, is closer to how it really is.

Your mental images were around this action of filling in the hole. Out of all the possible things that could be there, you related yourself to that one which included there being a spade at that place. It cannot be said that your mental attitude put the spade there, but it also cannot be said that your mental attitude had nothing to do with the spade being there.

The science of "materialising thoughts" and influencing the future is very important. Gurdjieff speaks about this in the "Fifth Descent" in *Beelzebub's Tales.* The Assyrian Hamolinadir has been to the "School of Materialising-Thought" in Egypt, the highest school of that time, but realises that something is missing. It is wonderful what Gurdjieff hides in that chapter.

You understand that I am saying that it is neither there nor not there. You are not seeing the future in the sense that the future is already there, but the potential future. By seeing it you make it become actual. If you had not seen it, the spade would not have been there.

S: Is this connected with planning and self-will limiting possibilities?

JGB: Oh yes. That is the other side of the picture. The kind of future where things can go right without effort is closed if you impose a plan on it.

S: J gave me an image for a cradle for his child. He gave me a verbal idea and I drew a picture in my mind. This is how I seem to work naturally with my hands on material things. But yesterday, being in charge of the house, I found I could not picture actual people doing the jobs. I could see the jobs that needed to be done and could picture them being done, but I could not put the person there. In the morning everything was fine but in the afternoon the mental image died. But things did come together.

JGB: The world of mental images and influencing the future and connecting oneself with what is happening—that world is not the world of our states. Our states are in a more superficial world. Sometimes we feel on top of the world and we can make mental images and so on and then everything collapses, and we are quite lost. Then one does not expect for a moment that things will go on working, but we see that they do. You begin to realise when you learn to work in this way, that all your changes of state, your ups and downs, do not matter.

S: With some mental images it seems just like a formality to carry them out; they seem to have been done already. There is a dangerous temptation in that. Also sometimes I have seen things in a mental image which I had not seen before when I am carrying them out.

JGB: You mean that some picture passed through your mind and you did not connect it with something actually happening?

S: Yes.

JGB: It isn't so common; it can happen once or twice in a week. You have something which looks like a sort of daydream and you don't think it has any meaning. You forget about it. Then later on, a day or two later, you find yourself doing something like picking up a heavy saucepan, and you remember, "Funny . . . I had this picking up of the saucepan before." This particular phenomenon was the basis of Dunne's *An Experiment with Time*, and we made experiments about this at Coombe Springs many years ago. One finds oneself doing something which is recognisably the same as something one had in a dream earlier. Time seems to have no importance and there does not seem to be any special purpose in it. It comes through sleeping dreams or through daydreams and the mental image is not made knowingly.

This is very important for understanding time better, but it has no value in the development of our powers.

S: There have been a number of times when someone has been speaking and I have become suddenly aware of the next thing that was going to be said. What came was a terrible fright, it is as if something terrible is going to happen. Is that of the same kind as you have been talking about?

JGB: Yes, but we need to talk about that separately, because we need to have a picture of what kind of things can enter the present moment. Some things enter from the future and there are moments when we actually see ourselves between two futures and this produces the sense of terror: will one fall into the hole?

S: I find that when I am breakfast cook and have to get up earlier and I visualise myself doing this the night before, I never have any difficulty. At other times, it doesn't work. When I am breakfast cook, I feel a sense of urgency and responsibility, a tremendous amount of feeling in a wish. I am very present when it is like that.

JGB: The mental image has to be given some body, some energy. It is not enough simply to have the picture. In the decision exercise, there is this crucial component—*one must not fail.* The feeling that one mustn't fail brings the necessary energy, and a real thought form is created which can connect with the unconditioned part of us, our *will.* You see, the thought form is made on level two and the decision on level three.*

When you have an external responsibility like being breakfast cook, the energy comes from that and you are able to have a genuine thought form. It is not just a state or something going through your mind: it has its own being apart from you and it will come and wake you up. You know how it is. You have the sense of meeting it and you realise that it is already there (when you come to take the action). When it is like that, you are no longer doing the action because when you created the thought form it was already done; it was placed in the future. Thought has the power of moving into the future which our bodies do not have. This power is not *thinking* about the future which does no good at all, it is a power by which we can actually move into the future as a thought form and find it when we get there.

---

*The reader can take this as it stands, but it is useful to remember that in this context, "level," amounts to much the same as "world." Level is used when there are distinctions of energy and world tends to be used when there are distinctions of law, such as more or less conditioned.

S: I have been doing the difficult part of *Shadze Vadze* (a Gurdjieff "movement") with my left hand. Last night I tried to do it with my right. At the beginning the arm was going down when it should have been up, so I said I want to try to make a mental image and have the sensation in my body of how I should do it. After doing that, I could do it much better. I'm wondering now if you could say something about the use and misuse of such a thing.

JGB: Teaching people about thought forms is a responsibility. If I had any fear that any among you would use this for magical purposes for the sake of power I would be very wrong to show you. I go with caution. I have not shown very much because this should only be given to people who have demonstrated that they have freed themselves from the desire for power. But what you talk about is very sensible and good.

The usual way in which people try to prepare themselves for the future or to learn things is to talk to themselves about it or to repeat something over and over again until they have learnt it. These are indirect ways that are slow. If you learn a thing by a thought form you have two advantages. One is that you can learn with all your centers in one. The other is that if you want to make a change, as in your example, it is very much easier to do than if you simply automatise yourself into one way.

S: I have difficulty putting this into words, but I will try. Last Thursday it came to me during the *zikr* in the morning that I should go back and do it again last thing at night, so I made a mental image of myself doing that. In the evening, after meditation when the day was over, I felt cold and tired and didn't want to do it at all. I found myself walking down the passageway towards the room when suddenly there was a kind of stop in myself. I realised that if I was committed and willing to this thing that was being done to me, what was really being asked of me was to go to that room, and <u>I saw that all the thoughts we had were really fantasies, unless there was a commitment to make them into some sort of reality</u>. I could see how helpless we all are in that and there was a fear that was really, really, painful . . . that it is like that with everybody in the world. At the same time there was an enormous feeling for everybody: we are really the same in that. It all happened in about thirty seconds and then I was just going on again.

JGB: Two things are very strange. One is that we are all helpless and don't know it, and the other is that we are not helpless and we also do not know that. As you say, people live in a fantasy where they neither see their mechanicalness nor the way out of it. This belongs to the Four Truths of Buddhism. You may know the words of it: this is *dukkha,* this is the arising of *dukkha* and this is the way to the cessation of *dukkha,* and so on. The word *dukkha* is hardly understood. What you described was the beginning of the seeing of *dukkha.* Sometimes people hear of the Four Noble Truths and think that they are dry and abstract and wonder how a religion could be founded on them. But when you begin to experience them, you see it is not like that. When "A" talked about her experience, I listened very carefully to see whether anything was being changed in the telling, and whether she was adding something of her own. When we see it is not our own, the seeing is something that is given to us.

This is the advantage we have of not using a set language. The word *dukkha* is ordinarily translated as "suffering," but that is quite wrong, suffering is only a secondary meaning. The word "helplessness" is most suited to what *dukkha* means. It is described sometimes as being carried along in the stream of *samsara,* helplessly carried; but one must experience this and see for oneself what it is that we have to escape from. Knowingly or unknowlingly, this is what you came here for—to learn the way to be free.

S: I have spent the time trying to track down one small thing about mental images. In the kitchen I was slicing some tomatoes for the pizza when it came to me: taste the soup. It was very, very, quick . . . a full blown thing, less like a visualisation than a prehappening of the thing. By the time I recognised it, I was across the room on my way to taste the soup. It seems that one of the problems with seeing these things is that they occur during a kind of break, during a kind of gap in between the actions, in between the attention and the things we do. It seemed to me that perhaps one way of dealing with this is to attempt to form mental images of the next events before this gap.

JGB: A thought form can arise full fledged like Athenae from the brow of Zeus. It can arise when we need it for the performance of some duty that we know about, but which might involve distracting influences. The thought form sees us through. It can arise because something in us becomes aware that something needs to be done and the thought form enables it to take shape. What was simply an indication acquires some substance, and the movement from indication to something substantial does require an action on our part.

We remain in the state of helplessness so long as we do not exercise that power of seeing and committing ourselves to the action that is indicated. But sometimes it all happens in this way with quite minor things. What is the condition for it to happen? I do not think that one can prepare for it because it works particularly when an unexpectedness arises. If you are in the right state, a mental image of something that has to be done in another room will arise and you will be drawn into that room. Then you will see why you were drawn there. You could not know it in advance. What we have to do is to keep ourselves in a state of alertness and sensitivity. This requires moral discipline. Without work on oneself sensitivity quickly goes, and we miss the indications that are coming to us. We become aware that we have lost touch and feel the discomfort of no longer being in contact with what is happening.

(Next came a discussion of the work of Matthias Alexander, in which people are trained to have their bodies following mental images instead of their habitual patterns. In this way postures are influenced which cannot be influenced by other means, especially not by so-called "voluntary" movements.)

S: Can you say something about the negative power of fantasy? I've noticed that if I want to destroy a possibility, all I have to do is to fantasise about it. If, for instance, I had nothing to say at this meeting and I did not want you to call on me, I would just fantasise about being called upon and say to myself that it won't occur. I've often used this in my life. It seems like an actual power, rather than coincidence or accident.

JGB: Yes, it does happen like that, but it is not reliable. You remember I spoke some time ago about expectation and how because of it we put ourselves under mechanical laws; we put ourselves into the mechanical future and very probably prevent the thing from happening. It is a matter of probability, it is not certain. By not expecting, we put ourselves into the line where the thing will happen. It is also true that in the fantasy world we are linked to deterministic or mechanical processes and therefore we will miss things which have a more conscious quality. What catches us into the stream of mechanical life, into *samsara*, is our refusing to face reality. We want the world to adapt to us. All the things that are described as "consequences of the organ kundabuffer" are the same as the arising and consequences of *dukkha*.

Even deliberately taking refuge in fantasy or daydreams is putting oneself into this helpless situation and from this, suffering comes. We go into that state simply in order to avoid suffering, but by making oneself helpless one is drawn into the situation where suffering becomes inevitable; and what is more, it is suffering that can only repeat itself. This is where we ourselves are responsible. No other power is responsible. There is nothing, not even God, that can give us freedom. Our Loving Creator can do no more than give us the possibility of freedom: our freedom then can be earned. Almost everything else can be given to us, but not freedom.

The Present Moment
(January 1966)

The present moment is our life, or our reality. Outside of this present moment there is certainly some greater reality, but we are not directly in it. Our present moment opens and closes. It can become very small, when all that is present is just some fragment of experience in a part of our nature. It can also open up and we can be directly aware of it doing so. In terms of consciousness, we can be aware of more or less, and it is possible to expand beyond our own experience and penetrate beyond this life or ours. People ordinarily think of the present moment in terms of consciousness, but the more important side has to do with *decision* and the will.

The decision that holds the present moment together is something that characterises every kind of being, but we men are given a certain power which enables us to live in a present moment far greater than that of any animal. We have memories of the past and we can forsee the future and have expectations. These memories and expectations of ours do not depend on the senses as do those of an animal, who anticipates or remembers because of the traces left in its organism of past sensations. We have something more than that. We are not brought together by the same kind of forces that bring animals together into a herd, or insects together into a hive. There is something in us which is able to make decisions because we can see the past and the future. This enables us to expand the present moment. That is why Gurdjieff said that a man was a being who can "remember himself." Not to be able to remember ourself is a sign of not being a man. In the chapter "Why men are not men" in Beel-zebub's Tales, Gurdjieff says that the reason is that they do not exercise the power of decision that is in them.

This does not mean that all the time we must live in a state of ex-panded consciousness, otherwise the present moment would be nothing else but a matter of consciousness. This is a mistake that is often made. It is often thought that our embrace of con-sciousness determines what we are, but this is not right. The present moment is not only what we are conscious of, but also what has become part of us by our own will and decision.

For example, if I decide to go for a walk, it is implied that I have two legs, that I have learned how to walk, that I have the strength to make the effort, and that I have the knowledge of how to get to the place I have chosen to walk to. None of these things need come into my awareness. The decision to take a walk covers all that is implied in my making such a decision.

We have met together to try to come to a new understanding of time. In this a whole lot is implied. One obvious thing is that you will be able to follow me when I speak in the English language. This is not consciously taken into account, but without it, this event could not be taking place. The present moment has some-thing of the nature of an iceberg—by no means is all of it floating above the surface where it can be seen. We are not aware of great deal of it. We can, by making an effort, become aware of something which is under the surface, but is usually not needed. There are some things, such as the finer workings of our organisms, that we cannot become aware of at all.

The present moment is the whole region of our experience with-in which we are able to do something—that is, where our ac-tions are connected with our purposes. Outside of the present moment we have to rely upon something external to make a connection. If I go outside of my present moment, there will be unknowables and unpredictables that can make it impossible for me to do even the simplest things. The realistic way of look-ing at the present moment is as the world of our effectiveness. Some people have a world of effectiveness that extends much further than it does for other people. We say that their respon-sibility is greater. Some people, for example, are able to take de-cisions which involve factors extending over months and even years. (That is, real decisions which are carried through.) Others can only take decisions which involve themselves and much smaller spans of time.

One part of our work is to learn how our present moment can be expanded, to go from a series of fragmentary experiences to the coherence in which we find ourselves. Another part of our work is to learn how the present moment can be shared, because the present moment of an individual shut up inside himself is really a very ineffectual thing.

When there is a complete cycle that can be forseen, as in these series of meetings, we can practise bringing our attention back to the purpose of it all. Doing this will in itself furnish enough data to begin to understand what I have said about the present moment. Such a practice is already work on enlarging our present moment and sharing with others. Real sharing comes through acceptance of a common pattern of *intention*.

What I am trying to get you to understand is the significance of *will*. But first of all we have to realise that will requires an instrument. It can be associated with any of the energies, which, so to say, enable it to work. But, according to the level of energy that will be greater or lesser freedom, and greater or lesser power of embrace associated with the present moment. When it is one of the lower energies working there are simply fragments of will. What I call the "automatic energy" manifests will as *many I's*: every thought, feeling and sensation saying "I." The fragmentation of will corresponds to the state of automatism in man. The automatic energy or substance does not permit an action of the will beyond the immediate experience of that part which happens to be experiencing. When there is a transition to the next level of sensitive energy, there is a sense of connectedness. It becomes possible to say yes or no. This is the first point at which the personal will begins to be operative. Beyond this point, real decisions are possible.

There is a combination of energies which produces a certain substance. When that substance is available, then the will is free to decide within the *whole* region into which the quality of stuff can penetrate. For example, if enough of this substance is in me, I can make a decision that will be (is) operative for the whole of myself. *The will is able, through that substance, to make a decision.* I am talking in almost literal terms—as literally as I can get it. There has to be "so much" of the substance because it is circumscribed and limited. It is quantitative, not just a quality of experience. When this substance is concentrated there is a present moment, and when there is a decision of the will that present moment is the present moment of that will.

We have certain exercises in our psychological work connected with acts of will and decision. You have to do something to prepare (perhaps not so much as an ounce, maybe a grain) some of this substance. Even one grain will enable you to make a decision that you will fulfil. This substance has the quality of certainty. When it works in the mind you can recognise truth. When it works in the feelings, you have positive emotions. It is through this substance that people are connected. When this substance is sufficiently concentrated in a group of people for the connection to be permanent, then this is what is called "the communion of the saints." In them, there is only one will. When this substance has actually pervaded the being of a person, they are transformed from an ordinary mortal to an immortal being.

This substance also enables us to be aware of destiny. When it is lacking, we have either to rely upon what we have received from tradition in the past of what people have done in similar circumstances, or we have to be guided and instructed. But when this substance is present and awakens the perception of destiny, then we do not require the one or the other; we see what has to be done. Jacob Boehme put it in this way, there are two "eyes" in man, one which looks into time and the other into eternity. For myself, I would say that the second "eye" looks into *hyparxis*, the direction of destiny, where something has to be accomplished in the creative world. We can see our destiny only to a certain point. Everything is limited.

As we are, our present moment is weak, but this is not solely a matter of our own weaknesses and limitations. There is a force which is trying to draw everything back into an undifferentiated state, or the *time state.* On the purely material level, this is just probability, but in the higher regions of energy it begins to take the forms of evil and temptation. The whole task of these forces is to disrupt the present moment so that a particular purpose should be accomplished. This is allegorically described in the Book of Job, where Satan is given special permission to disrupt Job's present moment until it is almost entirely destroyed. But something remains of his will, and although the substance of which we have been talking has been removed from him, his present moment is able to rebuild and return to all that it was, and more. It is quite accurate to picture the disruptive force on a high level as a conscious working. It is not just entropy. Job comes to see that although he does not lose his will, he is completely powerless and that his will depends on whether he is given the means to exercise it.

When the substance works in us we can *see.* It is an obligation for those who can see to help those who cannot. One who cannot see cannot do very much to help another one who cannot see. So, if two hundred people join together and none of them can see what is required, it will perhaps be two hundred times worse than if they operate separately. A mere joining together of people of good intentions guarantees nothing. The question we have in front of us is whether there are people who see and whether there are people who are able to take decisions on a scale that is great enough to form a present moment in which we can find our own place.

Most of the work we have done together has come from the transmission of something that I received and which has been transformed during the last twenty-five years of the activities to do with Coombe Springs. I was under an obligation to share this with you, because I received something that I had no doubt was the product of Work, of an understanding. But certain conditions remain unfulfilled; particularly conditions connected with this substance that I have been speaking about. It became quite clear to me that without this substance, one was bound to be ineffectual*. I long ago put aside the idea that one can work by one's own knowledge and natural abilities and strength alone. I had an experience with Gurdjieff in 1923 in which, under the conditions he was able to create, I was able to understand not only myself, but also him and what he was doing. That experience has remained unaffected by time and it is as strong now as it has ever been. At that time Gurdjieff was speaking about this substance and putting it in quantitative terms. He told us that we may not have enough of it for our work—we need a

---

*In Bennett's book, *Transformation* (Coombe Springs Press, 1978), the reader can find a broader description of the *help* that is needed to make our efforts effective and even to enable us to make the right kinds of effort.

pound but we have only an ounce. Then he said that some people have concentrated enough of it to have some to spare for others; then these others can become sources in their turn. All that he said was very vivid for me because I was experiencing the reality of it at that moment.

In the very same conversation that day, Gurdjieff spoke about "the Work" in an objective way, as a present reality which people who could recognize it were able to serve. It can only be served by those who understand what is required. The Work has its own present moment which is not the whole history of mankind and even less the happenings on the earth which are not even historical. In the world of happenings, possibilities go by the way of least resistance, according to the greatest probabilities. There is no resistance set up, or one so small that it only has the effect of producing little eddies that quickly disappear again. Then there are events in which a resistance is set up where people have strong convictions and are willing to make sacrifices. This produces a deep disturbance in the stream of happenings and builds something up, a potential that is not swallowed by time. We may not know the names of the people who produced the historical results, but we can recognise the event. The Work lies beyond this.

There is the possibility of seeing what has to be done, and this we call the Work. It must be clearly understood that there is no way of verifying the reality of the Work, because everything that we verify is only a result, and what is more, a second order result. The Work is effective in that region where our senses and our thoughts are blind, the region of destiny. One can ask why the purpose we are called to serve is not made plain to everyone, so that if we have the good will to do it we can serve it? But the serving of this purpose depends upon discovering it, not upon being told. What can be told belongs to the middle region where people see what they want to do and why they want to do it. The Work has a task to do just with that region in which men are blind, where they can only see if something is transformed in them; and this leads us again to the concentration of that substance without which we cannot see.

It is strange that we wish to do what is right; we wish to serve, but we are all stuck because we do not "see" what is required. We say "If only I knew what is required of me, even it meant the most bitter sacrifice, I could make it; but I cannot even make a sacrifice if I do not know what is wanted." It is because we do not "see" that we have this kind of undertaking, by which we try to prepare ourselves to come to the point where we will be able to do what is required. Until our own "seeing" comes, there is inevitable dependence. In the *Masnawi*, Jalal ad-din Rumi says, "If you have a lodestone then you find your own way, but if not, join with someone who has, otherwise your journeyings will be wasted."

It happens that if people join together in order to prepare themselves to see what is required, this very undertaking produces some of this substance, maybe enough for at least one person to "see." If one person "sees," it is enough, because they are so joined together that they know what has been seen is valid for them all. At this particular time, there is an enterprise of this kind going on. It depends on a decision that is not made by us, but by those who have the vision, who may not even be alive now. It is possible that this decision concerned this country, that here should be established a certain focus for the concentration of this substance to enable certain things to happen, rather like a service station. Such places have existed in different parts of the world, including Central Asia. It seems that several generations ago, at the beginning of the last century, some people saw that a certain kind of work had to happen in the West. There is a certain action, which may span two centuries, concerning a great transformation in the circumstances of human life on this earth. This action could not take place by people telling each other that the world was going through a crisis. It needs a great concentration of the substance we have been talking about, without which nothing can be done. It may be that the task of collecting this substance has been going on for a very long time. As some of you know, this task is often compared to the work of bees collecting honey, who gather it, drop by drop.

Possibly something of this sort has already been brought into the life of people, and this may account for some of the otherwise unaccountable events happening on the historical plane, such as people having been drawn together and accepting one another in spite of the frightful disruptive influences at work. This may be so. If it is, then what we are doing corresponds to that, but on a smaller scale and on a lower level of concentration. Because of the low level of concentration, it cannot produce the freedom of action that is required. The only way in which what we have done and are doing can be fruitful is if it is integrated into a larger action. Small actions make large actions possible, but they must be connected according to a permissible pattern. The honey can be collected and concentrated because the bees can also make honeycombs. Honeycombs are an analogy for various things, even places such as the one we have here.

When a new hive is to be started, the old hive has to make a sacrifice—sometimes it means even losing the queen. In the same way an extraordinary sacrifice has been made for what is happening now. I see more at this stage than you have been able to see. To bring the present moment into existence there has to be a separation. This is where something painful is involved and one must not suppose that it is otherwise. It may be that somewhere, for many centuries, there existed a place of concentration which produced, one can even say, blissful conditions of existence for those in its neighborhood, and the possibility of transformation for all those connected with it. It is a considerable thing to sacrifice all that and allow the concentration to move to another place. Without it, there could not be this event which we are seeing one corner of. We should have a special kind of gratitude towards the people who were ready to make such a sacrifice.

We know that when we try to work on our own it is very difficult. Each of us has a certain degree of commitment, which depends on this substance in us, but it is weak. We need to integrate ourselves into a present moment that is not just our personal decision. This is the significance of a group. Probably all of you who have worked in groups are aware of the difference between what you are able to do for the sake of the group and what you are able to do for your own sake. This is very surprising, considering how self-centred we are. It is strange that we really only care for ourselves and we are full of suspicions and difficulties in our relations with other people; and yet, when we come together in a group to undertake some kind of work, we find a force of quite a different order than the force we find when we try to work for our own sake. This can all be understood in terms of the present moment. The force of the individual will may be the greater, but the amount of substance that is available to make the will effectual is too little. When there are a number of people together there may be enough substance for a decision to be taken. If we can understand this in terms of our own experience of working in groups, we may then realise that on a larger scale, things may be possible which we do not dream of at the moment.

You must remember that I am talking about a direction within the present moment in which man is blind. It is not possible for me to produce evidence to convince you about these things. At best you can see by the results that something different has been at work, but you cannot tell what, or how it works.

The substance we have been referring to time and time again is not simply an energy like electricity, which requires a certain kind of apparatus in order to be useful; it is in itself an *intelligent energy*. At first it seems very hard to grasp that there is an intelligence which is not the intelligence of a person. But intelligence is a substance which enters into people and makes them intelligent. Without it they are not intelligent. In the ancient symbol of the honey and the bee, honey is the substance of intelligence, or the substance of "know-how," the substance by which it is possible both to see what has to be done and also to have the integrative power to make the necessary combinations in order to achieve it. The greater part of human life is run on an extreme minimum of this substance. A few people have it and are able to keep things going.

In Ouspensky's *Fragments* (In Search of the Miraculous), Gurdjieff refers to "knowledge" being limited. He says that it becomes dispersed and it is the duty of Schools to collect and concentrate this knowledge so that it can become available when required. This refers to knowledge, not in the sense of information, but in the sense of effectual knowledge or intelligence. When this is about, people act more wisely than they know. It is one of the most peculiar features of the twentieth century, especially now, that although dreadful things are being done and the disruptive forces are more dangerous perhaps than at any other time, there is a quite certain advancing towards a new state of affairs in the world—in which humanity will be able to accomplish things that have never been accomplished. This is not due to the cleverness of people, or to their good intentions, or to moral teachings—none of which could possibly prevail against the disruptive forces. What can prevail, if it is available, is this substance.

When this substance is available, it can produce actions in people which are more sensible than one would expect of them. This you can observe. When people know how to use it, it produces the action beyond history that we call the Work. It enables things to be prepared and the relation between fate and destiny to be rightly adjusted for humanity, so that things that have gone off the rails can be brought back and new tendencies introduced into human life. New modes of thought, new kinds of relationships and so on, are all possible if this substance is sufficiently concentrated in the hands of those who know how to make use of it. A great deal of the Work is concerned with this. To the extent that we can take part in this, we enter into this present moment.

Part VII

A man is incapable of perceiving the world in the way a woman does and neither can a woman perceive like a man. There are qualities of energies that a man can produce and qualities that a woman can produce and these require to be blended for a complete being to come. The higher significance of sex comes at this point. This is the act of will by which a man and a woman accept each other. It cannot come from our mechanical nature, it is an act of that part of us which alone can act and that is our will, our "I."

When a man and a woman look to each other and accept each other's burdens, we have the only thing that can be called marriage. Marriage cannot come until a man and a woman have evolved to the point where they are capable of making this act of will.

Uniqueness

Uniqueness belongs to the real world. It is not so remote. When one begins to put one's attention on it, one can begin to notice that one does have experiences that have the flavour of uniqueness. Then one can begin to recognise that it is not the repeated or knowable elements in our experience which are important; it is the unique and unrepeatable.

Our language is entirely based upon the repeated, the recognizable and the knowable. It is only by straining language or by using it with genius that it is possible to make an expression of the unique. This is one of the tasks of poetry, but there is always something that one still cannot express.

The real difference between the material and the spiritual is not that they are made of different "stuff," or that they are in worlds that are closed to one another. Materiality really means that which repeats itself without change. A stable atom may go for millions of years, tiny though it is, constantly repeating the same cycle of excited and unexcited states. And nothing else happens. It is entirely enclosed within its cycle of repetition. Life is more free, but when one goes beyond life, one enters the world of the unique where everything is what it is.

We allow ourselves to be caught by repetition and our language contributes very much to this imprisonment. At the end of the story of Moses and the Shepherd (*Masnawi,*) Rumi declares, "How often will you say, when the lid has been raised, 'This is not what I expected.'" If we are open to this then many things can enter.

Sameness*

Suppose we try to put this question, "Am I the *same* person?" and do not allow ourselves anything to make comparisons with, and treat the word *same* as if it meant something in itself. Then we have to ask, "But what is *sameness?*"

I can use various words with *ness* at the end of them— like human*ness*. I can recognise that there is a humanness in me; I can recognise that there is maleness in me. In other words I can recognise certain kinds of qualities that I share with some beings and do not share with others.

But what of this word *sameness?* I could try to make it easier for myself and put the word "as" in, as I am accustomed, and say, "Am I the same as myself?" At first it seems obvious to say, "Yes, of course I am." Am I? What kind of *sameness* am I talking about? Is this body the *same*—the *same* as the child that was born and took its first breath many years ago? Is it the *same* body? And if so, what do I really mean by that? If I say that now I am a person, a year ago I was a person, twenty years ago I was a person—and I am the *same* person? If I answer this yes, or no, what do I mean by *same?*

There is some *sameness* that we all share. Sometimes we say that "we are all the same." What is this sameness? Is is something that we arrive at by description? Are we the same in the

---

*In the last chapter of Gurdjieff's Third Series, *"The Inner and Outer World of Man,"* he refers to an ancient manuscript that discusses the contemplation of the sameness. He says, "Especially was I intrigued by the words, 'that which is the same'. What is 'sameness'? Why 'sameness'? For what purpose this peculiar 'sameness'?"

sense that we have two hands, two legs and two eyes, and one nose?

Suppose you try and ask yourself the question, "Am I the *same?*" You will be sure to find that this question will lead to strange answers. You will see beyond any doubt that you are not the same as you were a minute or so before—just the question coming into your mind has made you not the same. One thing that we have learned from self-observation is that we are not always the same. What about other people?

Is there not some way that I can say that I am the same as you are? We say that "We are all in the same boat." We have been talking about the collected state. The truth is that the collected state presents the same challenge to everyone. It is to succeed in separating oneself from everything until nothing at all remains. This is not only the same challenge, but it increases our *sameness* more and more as we go towards it. When we come to the collected state we are all the same.

In one way, we can say that we are all the same because we are all machines, we are all impermanent, we are all separate, enclosed within ourselves, shut off from our own inner reality, living in a dream. All people are the same in this way, but there is not real *sameness* there. All that that means is that we are all in the same boat, the same predicament. But the other kind of sameness is reached when we are emptied to a state of pure consciousness. This is the same *sameness,* no divisions, no distinctions, the pure *sameness.*

The word *sameness* can be used from the outside. We speak about, "like as two peas in a pod," where the peas have the same shape and the same potential, the same colour and much the same size. And then there is the same *sameness* looked at from within. They are a whole infinity apart.

There is a deeper *sameness* we have than simply being in the same predicament. Gurdjieff constantly uses the phrase "children of our Common Father," which says that we all have the same origin, come from the same Source. That *sameness* can begin to be real for us—the sameness of origin and the sameness of destination. It is quite different from the *sameness* of pure-consciousness, and it is quite different from the external sameness of form and function. We discover that our identity is by no means a definite fixed thing. We begin to discover a part of us in other people and a part of them in us. The notion of identity begins to change and we see that *sameness* is something bigger. If we work on this it will help us with what we have to do now, which is to learn how truly to recognise other people and how to accept them by seeing the *sameness* that there is in us and them. In words there is a fictitious sameness. You will remember in the last chapter of *Beelzebub's Tales*, Gurdjieff talks about the difficulty of people understanding one another. He gives an illustration that people use the word "world" and each person who uses the word will mean something different by it. So it is no use saying the word "world" is the same word— it is only sameness in external form. If we human beings were the same in that way it would not amount to anything.

Gurdjieff in the *Science of Idiotism* insists on the necessity of returning to the point where we completely accept that we are the same as other people. That is what is meant by ordinary idiot— ordinary-same. If we do not start from there, sooner or later we will be caught out, and perhaps so caught, that it is almost impossible to escape. At some point we have to be naked; having nothing, carrying nothing with us. At some point, in order to pass through, we must have nothing at all; and if we have not learnt how to have nothing at all we shall be stuck there. It is also true that from that point* onwards, there is more and more individuality until we come to the summit of all things, the *Unique Idiot,* as it is in the Qu'ran. "Say that God is unique."

The trouble with us is we want to have the *sameness* that belongs to God, while we are still very far away from God and very far from any notion of what it costs to be God. We do not understand what a blasphemy it is to think that we are unique— because it really means that we think we are God. Only God is unique. Yet this is the goal. This is the direction. As we mount the scale of being, identity becomes more and more marked. I have been exceptionally fortunate in the number of very outstanding spiritually developed men that I have met. Every one was unique. This does not mean that they were God, I mean unique in a human sense, totally unlike the others. Ordinary people are not like that.

*It is unclear from the talk whether he is talking here of the ordinary idiot or some "higher" point, such as the enlightened idiot, from where we must "consciously descend."

In the ordinary levels of being, "same" means "same as." One pea is the same as any other pea and, even to a considerable degree, one man is the same as another man. But when we go further there is *sameness*, not "same-as." Then we have that peculiar thing beyond understanding, we go beyond the distinction between one and many, and we are no longer able to say "this is the same as that," because it would imply that there were two things. Why is it said that all the great prophets are the *same?* Why, when Gurdjieff talks about Cosmic Individuals, does he say they are the *same?*

Gurdjieff's Science of Idiotism is about the transformation, step by step, from the mechanical sameness which really is an *absence* of identity, to the other sameness which is the *perfection* of identity. One of the perils of this path is that one can take oneself as having a kind of identity, a kind of reality, that one has not got. Living with this illusion it comes to the point where it is impossible to get any further.

There is one aspect of sameness that we have to be on our guard against, and this is called "identification." The state of identification belongs to World 96*, to the world of illusion. It cancels out whatever positive thing there may be. There may be something positive, but if we become identified it all leads to nothing. The whole thing is nullified. We have sympathy with someone and this is good and necessary. It is necessary to know what real sympathy is—taking somebody else's suffering into ourselves.

But how is this to be done? How do we deal with our own suffering? By becoming free from it. If we understand our suffering, we see it is this body that is suffering, it is this personality. I must be free. I am free. There is nothing that I am touched by in this. Not that one must cease to suffer. Not at all. One must be able to suffer objectively, not subjectively. If someone is suffering one must have the wish to take that person's suffering into oneself. The freedom one has in relation to one's own suffering one must have in relation to another's suffering. Otherwise it is no good at all. The suffering will not be transformed in us and neither we nor the person who is in distress will be benefitted by it.

---

*"World 96" means the world subject to ninety–six laws, half of which are negative. This is the world in which nothing real can happen. The various worlds are described in Bennett's book, *Deeper Man*, Turnstone Press, 1978.

Identification is the falsification of sameness. This is where it goes to hell. So you see, there is natural samenss, which is ordinariness; there is divine *sameness* which is uniqueness; and there is also this diabolic sameness that is identification. Identification sucks the life out of everything.

The Lord's Prayer*

"Be ye therefore perfect as your father in heaven is perfect."
This extraordinary saying at the end of the Sermon on the
Mount is such a shock. How can we be expected to be not only
perfect, but to be as perfect as our Father in heaven? Represented at point nine, "Our Father" is the source of our perfection. If we are able to be in tune and at one with the Will of the
Father, then our actions can be perfect. This is *doing*.

"Thy Kingdom come." In both the Beatitudes and the Lord's
Prayer, point three represents the work which has to be done
here in this world. The kingdom of heaven should come here.

"Forgive us as we forgive them. . . ." Here at point six we
have a very strange thing. The forgiveness of sins is the preroga-
tive of God. It is not for men to forgive sins. We do not know the
hearts of people and we do not know who should and who
should not be forgiven. Yet here it is said that we should undertake the task of forgiving. How is this possible?

It is possible because God is in our hearts. We have a will which
God has placed in us, who are his children. Therefore we can
forgive. This is our real spiritual work. Forgiveness is the releas-
ing of men from their bondage. In Northern Buddhism it is said
that when a man has achieved liberation and becomes a Bodhisattva, his compassion forbids him to leave this existence as
long as there are creatures still in bondage. The same reality is

*This is part of a talk on the *enneagram* of the Lord's Prayer and it is complementary to the talk on the *enneagram* of the Beatitudes that was published in
Needs of Future Communities, (Coombe Springs Press, 1977). The principles of
the *enneagram* are explained in the book of that name, published by Samuel
Weiser, 1980.

expressed here in the Sermon on the Mount and is in the prayer we make for forgiveness "as we forgive."

Forgiveness has to be total, not only of a part. There has to be such a complete love of mankind that we forgive all that has been done to bring us into bondage with this world. Even when we attain liberation and *our* trespasses are forgiven, we still remain with the task of forgiveness. This is essentially a spiritual inner work. It is not something that we are required to do outwardly because, as I said, we cannot know what we are doing. Our forgiveness of men must be from the heart, from within. There must be such a total and impartial love that it is impossible for us at anytime to think of other men as outside or as different from us. We should feel with truth that we love our neighbor as ourselves.

Such is the meaning of it. We should ask forgiveness as we forgive. There should be no difference, not only between us and other men, but also between us and God. We should do the same work as God does: as He forgives and when we forgive it is He in us that is forgiving.

This is how we should look at point three, six and nine. Now what is the meaning when we go round one, four, two, eight, five, seven?

The first thing to understand is that God the Father is not here in this state of existence. We shall not find God as God walking on the earth. We shall not find God as God speaking to us. God is "in heaven." That means that God is in a state beyond existence. It is a state in which we ourselves belong; but as long as we are in existence it is inevitable that we should be subject to separation. There can be visions, there can be illuminations, there can even be revelations to us men; but this does not mean that we can see God giving evidence of His presence in this world.

It is emphasised from the very start that we have to relate ourselves to God "in heaven." This leads us to the working of God's Will (from point one to point four), "Thy will be done on earth as it is in heaven." What is beyond this conditioned state of existence with a will that is to manifest here on earth. We have the union of heaven and earth represented at point four. It is an act of will. We should realise that this is what we are born for: we should be the means by which the Will of God should be done on the earth.

"Hallowed by Thy Name." At point two we come to the name of God. This is the name "God." The name by which we address God is the name "Father" and we have said "Our Father." It is necessary for us to realise that this is what we are talking about: God as Father. We are not talking about God as Creator, God as King and ruler of the world; nor God as omnipotent; but God as Father. The fatherhood of God is very much the concern of the whole of the Gospel of St. Matthew. Here it is made so clear and emphatic that we must look at this blessed name "Father" and realise that we are related to God in this unique and extraordinary way—as children are to their father. If we do not understand this, then we do not understand anything about the intention of the whole Gospel, nor about the intention of Christianity. Christ is constantly trying to bring home to his disciples that they are to look upon God as their father; not as judge or ruler or creator, but as father.

God our Father has the characteristics of father: he is engendered in us; part of Him has entered into us. That name we should have constantly in us. This was most strongly brought home to me twelve or fifteen years ago when I was serving mass for the father Abbot at St. Wandrille. It was the Mass of the Immaculate Conception and we were given a fair time after the mass to pray in silence. During that time it came over me so clearly and strongly (that I can never forget it) that one must understand that it is extremely important, and to be taken quite literally, that God is in the relation of father to us and that all other relationships are not the significant ones. God has given part of Himself to us, as a father gives part of himself to his own child.

It is for this that we should praise and give thanks to God, and we have "the kingdom and the glory" at point eight. It is for this reason that the coming of the kingdom is important. The kingdom is not the kingdom of an omnipotent ruler who has no need of us; it is the kingdom of a father who would think it useless to bring his kingdom and leave his children out of it.

Then we have to realise that something should come to us from God that we need all the time. "Give us our daily bread," as point five, represents the blessing or *baraka* that we need incessantly, not just once, daily, hourly. It is the means by which the spiritual life is made possible for us. It comes to us because power is with God; because we are destined for the kingdom and because man is destined to manifest the glory of God on earth.

Next we go to the crux of the practical work. We ask, "Deliver us; lead us not into temptation." In the Greek version it says "deliver us from the evil one" and not deliver us "from evil." The "evil one" is our own egoism. Here represented at point seven is our final liberation and we are in need to achieve it.

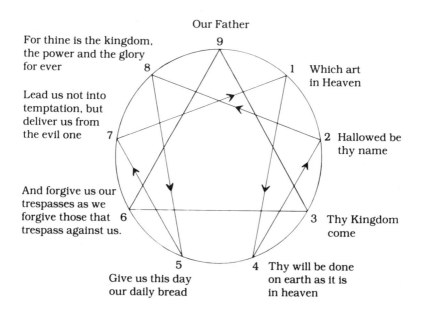

Enneagram of the Lord's Prayer

Book Two

The Octave
of Salvation

Introduction to Book Two

The writings that follow are my compilation from notes that J.G. Bennett made in 1944. They constituted the final chapter of a book Bennett was writing on the "System" of Gurdjieff. As he writes in his autobiography *Witness*, it was a decisive time in his life, when he stood alone and had no devise to find his own way.

I have taken many liberties with the originals, but tried to identify those bits which are my own. These notes, made thirty years before the meetings recorded in the first part of this book, can be looked at as the theory behind the practical efforts of the succeeding years. Those unfamiliar with Gurdjieff's terminology should not be put off by unusual use of words. The ideas here are startingly simple—if the reader really wants to know them.

Put it in a nutshell, the main idea is that there is a complete organic whole of evolving humanity. If a man or woman so will, they can participate in this whole. The wish and efforts that can awaken in a man or woman can bring them to the point at which a real journey into their own essential self can begin. What lies ahead is perhaps unlimited. It cannot be predetermined. An unknown number of great human souls who have 'gone far ahead' are with us on this Earth here and now and through them we are helped in our own work of salvation.

A. G. E. Blake
Daglingworth
December 1979

Dilemmas

July 1944

The question 'what shall I do to be saved?' presupposes the recognition of what constitutes 'salvation'; but, in reality, salvation is one of the most difficult conceptions to define. The Christian idea of salvation is essentially 'other wordly': "What shall it profit a man if he gain the whole world and lose his own soul?" "Whosoever will save his life shall lose it." "Lay not up for yourselves treasures upon earth. . ." This teaching that the present world - if not a vale of tears - is, at any rate, no more than a vale of soul-making, with no values of its own, permeates Christian thought and constitutes the principal link between Christianity and the other-wordly religions of the East, particularly Buddhism.

Against such views of salvation as requiring liberation from desire for this world, is the deep-seated interest of almost the whole of mankind in this world and its temporal processes and values. Are we to conclude that the great masses of mankind are entirely deluded as to their true welfare, or is there some middle way suggested by the words "seek ye first the Kingdom of God and His righteousness and all these things shall be added unto you"? "*All* these things" seems to mean that all the values of the world can be redeemed and retained providing they are given their due place: subordinate to the things and values of the Kingdom of Heaven. The same is implied in: "Render unto Caesar the things that are Caesar's and unto God the things that are God's."

What can we learn about salvation from the teachings of our system?

The words "our system" refers to the integrated psychological and cosmological view of man, the world, and God, which was introduced by Gurdjieff. Gurdjieff conveyed by a multitude of ways a *vision* (in Sanskrit *darshana* or "view") *of the whole*. A major part of the system was based on understanding universal laws applying on all scales. Two such great "common cosmic laws" were the *law of three* and the *law of seven*. By the "law of three" is meant the harmonious movement lying hidden behind the clash of opposites. By the "law of seven" is meant the vision of how all things come to their completion and fulfillment. In the "system" the relationship between man and the cosmos is described very exactly; but in such a way that it has to be made substantial and real by an understanding that arises from within the individual in his work of transformation.

It is itself neither more and certainly not less than a scheme of salvation. The very idea of man as an undeveloped being implies that there is something better and higher through which he can be 'saved'. At the same time the nature of salvation appears complex and ill-defined. From one point of view it is fully expressed in the doctrine of the Seven Categories of Man. Only man No. 7 can be called 'saved' in the fullest sense of the word.

The teaching of seven categories of man is a based on the axiom that men are not alike and also differ in their *level of being*. Men number 1, 2, and 3 refer to ordinary untransformed men, who are to be characterized by a bias in their functions toward sensations, feelings and thoughts respectively. Until these are brought into balance with each other, such a man cannot develop in his understanding and experiences in an undistorted way. Man No.4 is a balanced man. He marks the transition to higher levels of being without existing on a higher level himself. Man number 5 has realized his own essence: he is the true individual *in his own right*. Sometimes Gurdjieff describes him as a "sacred individual" to emphasize that this individuality entirely comes from within and is not dependent on external events. Man number 7 realizes what lies beyond the creation altogether; he is united with the Source, or *Shiva*.

The idea that there exist on Earth superior beings in human form is common to all traditions without exception. Saints, saviours, *avatars, abdals, arahants,* prophets etc. - such are the words that have been used. Gurdjieff largely avoided all traditional terminology and presented his scheme of Seven categories of Man in an abstract way, leaving it to conscious disciples of the future to understand the ramifications of the existence of an hierarchy of transformed and nonordinary beings here on this Earth.

The point in such teachings is not to give cut and dried explanations but the principles through which understanding could grow in a right, balanced way.

He alone has passed beyond all possibility of failure in space, time and even eternity. His Will is united with the Absolute Will and he is free from the Laws of All Worlds. But Man No. 7 is a mythical Being, whose very existence in a given epoch is unknowable. * He is rare.

There must be more meaning to 'salvation' than the perfect achievement of one individual in ten thousand million. The main difficulty of Christian doctrine - as in all human thought on great questions and small - is the hidden tendency towards an irreconcilable dualism, which contains the seeds of its own dissolution. For Christians a man is either 'saved' or 'not-saved'. Even the Purgatory and Limbo of the medieval Catholics are not a 'third' state but an attempt to soften the contradictions of an uncompromising division into Paradise and Inferno.

All schemes of 'salvation' in Christian and other religions are dualistic in their essence, but tempered with various artifices in an attempt to meet the absurdity of dividing the infinite range of human values sharply into two categories. It is instructive to note the common trend towards an optimistic solution. Through the doctrine of reincarnation the Eastern religions find a way of reconciling the evident failure of this life with a belief in the ultimate liberation of all beings. Christianity and Islam look for hope of salvation for all but a few damned souls notwithstanding the exactly contrary assertions of their Founders, such as: "Many are called but few are chosen." The oversimplification of all dualistic thought is seen in the soteriological doctrines of all churches and it is only possible by recognizing the triadic character of human destiny to find a conception which is free from contradiction and from the omission or neglect of the most evident data of our experience. The most certain fact about mankind is that none are all good or all bad and that there is no clear hierarchy of values in which a division can be made. Not only are men various, but a single man is himself a multiplicity and the 'many' in him can neither merit nor enjoy all the same destiny.

We must account for the many different levels in man as well as for the variety of types.

---

* Perhaps Bennett is being too cautious here. It is a question of Revelation, whether the highest being is known or not. In our own time, the living stream of the high Hindu tradition name Him as *Dakshinamurti*, Shiva, who resides on Mount Kailasa in the Himalayas.

According to our system, man's destiny cannot be conceived except in relation to the worlds in which he lives. From one point of view it can be said that his destiny is to be liberated from the laws of the lower worlds in order to live in the higher worlds. This is true, but it cannot be the whole truth, for man himself is not all of the same substance and there are parts of him which, by their very nature, can live only upon a certain level. Are those parts, for example, which belong to the earth and can only live upon the level of the earth, to be discarded? Or, at any rate, are they to be looked upon as 'not self'; as an inferior vesture to be put off as soon as the 'wedding garment' of a higher world can be procured? ". . . now I am become a man I have put away childish things?"

According to this view, although there is not exactly a dualism such as the saved and damned, there is an unique sequence. This seems at variance with the complexity and fullness of life. "If they love a weed, albeit an amaranthine weed, suffering no flowers save its own to mount?"

Are we to have regard only to what is highest and most perfect in ourselves and to look upon all other parts of our being as valueless, or at any rate as possessing value solely in so far as they can serve the highest? This is the religious view and it has been accepted unreservedly by some of the greatest and best of men.

Mystical experience points to a supreme state in which all other values are drowned in the realisation of the Divine. But this experience is rare even in the lives of those who have enjoyed it. It does not explain the world, but destroys the need for it.

The crucial question for mystical experience is whether these rare moments are all that matter and whether the rest of life is a mere preparation for their arrival. The answer of nearly every mystic to this question is that life does not matter and that service to God is as necessary as knowledge of God. But there is no explanation of the relation between the two lives. Martha and Mary are seen as complementary and necessary to one another, but for the non-mystic their relations appear to be artificial and even meaningless. If direct participation in Divine experience is to all other values as infinity to zero, for what can *works* serve but the purgation of all that obstructs that participation?

The issue of withdrawal from the world versus the service of mankind concerned Bennett very much and he tried to resolve this problem in his discussions with the Nepalese saint, Shiva Puri Baba (*Long Pilgrimage,* Turnstone Press, 1975, gives an account of the Saint's teaching and his answers to such questions). The Shiva Puri insisted that the first task was to seek knowledge of God. The implication was, that in this knowledge duties and service no longer affect the state of withdrawal.

Gurdjieff's dictum was: *first* be an out and out egoist (save yourself) and then you *will be able* to be an altruist.

There is here a dualism which leads to the cleavage between the active and the contemplative lives. If inward experience of God is all in all, then the outward life of virtue must be subordinate and no reason for it can remain once the soul is liberated from the veil which obscures the vision. But if our destiny is to serve God and not to experience Him, then the contemplative life may be an evasion of our duties, or at best, a source of strength and inspiration to support us in difficulty and trial.

Here are some of the questions we have to face.

- Religions teach that salvation is by the Grace of God. If it is true, what is our role in this? How can we understand the meaning of spiritual work?

- Salvation is often pictured as coming into a life in an 'other world'. If we deny ourselves the convenience of putting the other world into an imaginary space after death, what does getting into another world mean?

- If we picture salvation as a present state how is this consistent with a continuing existence on Earth?

- Salvation need not be exclusively theistic. The Samkhya tradition of *liberation* like the Buddhist is usually considered to be non-theistic. The Yoga sutras use the term *kaivalya.* What is the state of liberation for the self? Is there a state beyond individuality?

- Is the whole man saved or only his 'soul'? What place does his body have in salvation?

- Are only a few saved or is there an ultimate salvation of all souls?

Earthly Life

It must be clear from all that has gone before that the dualistic ideas of salvation which are current in nearly all religious systems are false. There can be no clear cut division between salvation and damnation, between life and death. This is the most important and the most difficult idea to accept. No man can be perfectly saved - no man can be completely lost. There is not, however, merely an infinite gradation in the possibilities which are open to each man. Also, according to the system, each Essence has its own fate and its own salvation.

So long as we live on the Earth and our consciousness is centerd mainly in our physical bodies, in other words, so long as the center of gravity of our being is H48, we are bound to the Laws of the Earth and we must recognize and submit to the consequences. There can be no certainty, no permanence, no moment when we say, 'now I am safe, I need no longer be on my guard'.

This also means that there can be no guarantee of salvation. We can only look for probabilities and not certainties. Life in time and space is governed by laws of probability, not laws of certainty, and we must try to increase the probabilities of right states and decrease the risk of bad states by the use of right methods and by seeing right conditions of work.

Man on Earth is drawn by the opposing forces of the Planets and the Moon.

The Moon stands for the forces of delusion and the Planets for the forces of a man's potential. In the 'System', a parallel objectivity-subjectivity of cosmos and man is asserted. 'Moon' and 'Planets' are not just psychological metaphors. Later on, Bennett will refer to the 96 laws of the Moon and the relatively free state of the 24 laws of the Planets.

The one force draws him towards the realization of his own fate, the other towards the dissolution of his individual existence. Only life on Earth is subject to the Laws of Time and Space and to the separateness in which conflict is possible. It is only by conflict that a new life can be created. Salvation upon Earth is, in one way, the most difficult of all to understand because it is nearest to us and we are confused by the multiplicity of values with which we are beset.

Salvation of Earth consists in the full realization of our creative powers, whatever form they may take; in breaking down the barriers which separate us from the natural world in which we live and in gaining power of free choice.

Whatever may be the attainment of a man in his life on Earth it can only be 'safe' by constant adjustment. In our life on Earth, we are subject to the negative influences from which we cannot isolate ourselves except by withdrawal or by entering a School.

The man *himself* cannot be saved through life on Earth. The salvation of 'he himself'—*his essence*—is not in time, but in *eternity*. In realizing himself, a man becomes what he is, but this is not along the line of his earthly life. Essence is saved by its becoming. We can think of this as the whole of salvation, but it is not the whole story, just as fulfillment of earthly life is not the whole of salvation.

Salvation and Realization

The usual attempts in religion to deal with salvation can be reduced to the simple formula: 'saved,' 'damned,' and 'x.' This is totally unreal and artificial and we should look for the real dynamic of the situation. For this we need to understand man's *becoming* in a very deep sense. We can conceive becoming only as a process in time, but there must be an aspect which is universal and beyond time and even eternity.*

There is nothing in a man's external activities which is *necessarily* opposed to his becoming, except through over-emphasis or wrong valuation. This is one meaning of the words: "Render unto Caesar that which is Caesar's." and "I have not come to destroy but to fulfill". There is, however a deeper significance in our life on earth that is connected with our *self realization*. This is to do with our eternal reality.

In the path of salvation there appears to be a very sharp dualism. The Gospels say: "He that is not with me is against me". "He that shall save his life shall lose it". "No man can serve two masters". The opposites here serve the practical need of establishing a *direction* of becoming. They do not refer to static conditions but to the moment of inward action.

Salvation must be broadly understood in the religious sense, *but not to the exclusion of other values.* Salvation is not merely a passage *from* one stage *to* another, but the progressive realiza-

---

*What Bennett was searching for here was another dimension like time but involving no process. This is the dimension people call *realization*, which we can first of all grasp as the moment of understanding. Bennett in his later writings *The Dramatic Universe* called it *hyparxis*—"ableness to be".

tion of the possibilities inherent in each world truly belonging to man. The realization of a higher possibility does not destroy but enriches the results of lower ones.

Man as a being is what he is, like everything else is what it is. He exists and has a place in the whole. Salvation is not an issue here. Nor is it an issue in the divine reality of love. There is Love equally for all things. This is the nature of the unitive energy of Love.* Through Love we may be saved; but *in Love there is no movement of salvation.* Salvation applies only to man's becoming.

---

*c.f. J.G. Bennett, *Energies*, Coombe Springs Press, 1978, for an account of the hierarchy of energies. He was greatly influenced not only by Gurdjieff but also the theology of the Eastern Church

The Octave of Salvation

The whole process of salvation as the becoming of Man is an inward and outward integration. Becoming is the simultaneous growth of inward independence and freedom and of outward relations and dependencies. The whole process is organic. It is the timeless realization of a *whole,* not a passage from one temporal state to another. The transformation can however be conceived and studied as a process and therefore must be seen as an ascending octave. The octave falls into two parts linked by an interval:

Preparation	Do	The Birth of Discrimination
	Re	Finding the Way
	Mi	Realization of Own Nothingness
Interval	☐	Help and Decision
Fulfillment	Fa	Acceptance of the Way
	Sol	Right Living, Man No.4
	La	Realization of Self, Man No.5
	Si	Union with the Great Self, Man No.6
	Do	Final Liberation, Man No.7

Each stage takes different forms according to the characteristics of the individual. The stages are not necessarily successive. Each individual has the form of salvation appropriate to himself. His own choice and decision are an essential element in salvation. At the same time man grows progressively less and less isolated from his fellow men. In the higher levels there is actual unity of being.

The stages of fulfillment correspond to the Laws of the Worlds.

Fa	Acceptance of the Way	= Work against Laws of Moon	World 96
Sol	Right Living	= Fulfillment of Laws of Earth	World 48
La	Realization of Self	= Freedom in Laws of Planetary World	World 24
Si	Union with Great Self	= Laws of the Sun	World 12
Do	Final Liberation	= Freedom from all incomplete triads by entry into Laws of	World 6

Beyond World 6, there is no form of existence for which the words 'Man' or 'individual' have any meaning.

Preparation brings us to the point at which salvation becomes a real possibility; but at that point a step has to be made that is not a natural consequence of what has gone before. That is why we speak of an *interval,* meaning that there is a change of tempo requiring a new kind of energy to go further. All that, previously, has been simply known about can become *practical;* instead of talk and mental experience alone, a real journey can begin, a journey unique to every individual engaged on it but universal in its form.

Salvation of the Essence (la) means to become fully and eternally myself. This is the link which I myself must forge and the work which no-one else and no external forces can do for me.

The Mystic who tries to reach the Jesus state (si) without first becoming himself remains with the essence of his work undone.

To become myself, I must learn to choose always what is right for me. But it is not 'becoming oneself' a wrong expression of the work of 'crystallisation' of which G. speaks? Surely he implies that something new and different appears? No, for the analogy of the metallic powders shows that it is the same material, the *same substance* which is fixed into permanent unity.*

*c.f. P.D. Ouspensky, *In Search of the Miraculous,* Routledge and Kegan Paul, 1972, p.43

Then what is 'sacrifice'? It is not the sacrifice of the real, but of the false. A man must constantly resist the attractive force exerted on him by the Moon. This keeps him fluid. The moon prevents his own self from forming.

How can we recognize the attraction of the Moon? This is the work which corresponds to *fa* in the Octave of Salvation.

If we speak of stages of salvation, then:

DO	To know what I want
RE	To find out about the way
MI	To recognize the inherent difficulties
☐	To decide to work
FA	To work against the Moon
SOL	To live rightly on Earth
LA	To realize my essential being
SI	To be united with Jesus
DO	To penetrate beyond the veil of individual Existence.

The failure of ordinary life is never to cross the interval after *mi*.
The failure of orthodox religion is that it stops at *fa*.
The failure of mysticism is due to ignorance of the stages *sol* and *la*.

As we conceive it, the domain of fulfillment (fa-sol-la-si-do) is centred in self realization. Below this comes right living, or harmony in the domain of existence, and above comes union and annihilation, or harmony with what is beyond existence. We must become ourselves before we can become other. But we cannot become ourselves without help for we cannot separate the false from the true.

The *whole octave* is *the way*.

Preparation (do-re-mi)

DO. *Conversion.*
More generally the formation of magnetic center*. The realization of being in an 'unsaved' state, which leads to the discrimination between 'transient' and 'permanent' values. The birth of the desire for becoming. The transition from unconscious to conscious becoming. 'The first Awakening'.

RE. *Striving.*
Finding the way. School conditions as external.

A School is an organization of help or teaching from a higher level (we leave out of account all the many pseudo-schools) and can take any form. Here the meaning is that the individual is connected only as a physical being, externally; his heart is not awakened to the reality.

Work under domination of negative triad.

The negative triad is that by which all our efforts come to nothing. It signifies that we are locked in to a distorted pattern of perception and response which keeps us just as we are, so to say running on the spot. The more we strive to be free, the more this distortion in us comes to the fore. We begin to experience it but cannot overcome it.

Selfwill unconquered. Learning. First glimpses of possibilities. Experiences of higher states. Work on three lines.

The lines are: work for oneself, work for the group and work for the world. P.D. Ouspensky, *The Fourth Way,* Routledge & Kegan Paul Ltd., 1972, pp. 268-92.

*Magnetic centre (a Gurdjieffian term) in a man is a pulling or being called towards the truth. It is the first real stirring of his movement towards the Source.

Realization of need for others.

MI.   *Purgation.*
The realization of failure as due to oneself only. Understanding of self-will. The force of the negative triad at its maximum. Recognition of absence of 'decision'. Inability to receive help. Realization of own nothingness in comparison with aims and obstacles. Certainty that no compromise will avail. 'The Second Awakening'.

This leads to the state in which the way becomes clear and unmistakable, and no doubt remains that all other desires must be sacrificed if it is to be followed. Rejection of *isolation.*

Interval

This is the shock in the octave of salvation. External conditions now take the form of conscious help. Self-will is broken down. The cry is 'Lord save us, we perish'. 'Not my will but Thine be done'. Bargaining and compromise no longer avail anything. The inward decision is seen as helplessness. 'By myself I cannot do anything and never will do anything, but I will cooperate with Thy Will to the limit of my strength'. Acceptance, joyful acceptance, of anything which will lead on to the *Way*. This stage is seen to be one in which the illusion of inner decision is abandoned and yet that very decision which of itself is worthless becomes all-important as the complement of 'grace': the paradox of religion. G. on "standing on one's head".

There is no salvation until this stage has been accomplished. But it may be sudden or gradual according to type and school, and method of work. It is not specifically religious.

Stages of Fulfillment
(fa-sol-la-si-do)

FA.   *Salvation from the Laws of the Moon.*

This is the first Salvation because it is the key to all others. I am saved from the Laws of the Moon as soon as my attitude towards the negative triad is permanently established. This means that I must cease for all time to justify imagination, self-love and identification. I cannot guarantee that these negative triads will never appear in me, but I must never permit willingly that they should remain.

In relation to *imagination*, I must be ready at all times to face reality, to accept the truth about myself and my state. I must reject all ideas such as 'if things were different I would be different etc. . .'

In relation to *self-love*, I must sacrifice all suffering caused by my false own valuation of myself. I must not willingly permit any negative state or attitude towards anyone or anything.

In relation to *identification*, I must desire freedom. I must decide with all my heart that I wish to live in a higher world, even at the cost of effort and sacrifice. I must look upon 'sleep' as altogether bad.

Each of these requirements involves a decision. This decision cannot be taken once and for all, but must grow slowly in us. Every day we must renounce afresh the forces of the Moon and every night we must renew our attitude. But the real work consists in finding our own weaknesses and above all our own chief weakness. It is only through mastering our own 'chief feature' that we can be *saved* from the Moon.

The greatest fight of all is against the Imaginary 'I'. This is the enemy of Jesus. It must be understood clearly that the salvation so far won is only kept by struggle. It slips away whenever we weaken. But it can always be found again when we put away our self-will. In this stage there are fluctuations of state. The amplitude of the fluctuations depends upon the type and conditions. Usually there are direct experiences of higher states of consciousness which presage the fuller salvation to come. There may be moments of real knowledge of the Self - the Master - Jesus. There will also be failures when all seems to be lost.

This stage is described by mystical writers as 'drymen' or 'light'. The true character of this stage is that it is the *conversion of the act of decision into a permanent freedom from the Laws of the Moon.*

Acceptance of the way. This comes from permanent *attitude.* Knowledge of right and wrong. Decision is constant renewal of *attitude.* Attitude of 'the whole mass of oneself' compared with partial attitudes.

SOL.   *Salvation on Earth.*

This is a state of equilibrium. It requires a constant adjustment. We need three things to be saved:

1. right attitude
2. right work
3. right conditions

Right attitude means understanding that our purposes must correspond to real values if we are to be safe. There is mortal danger in all aims which go contrary to our fate.* Therefore we must know our fate, or accept the guidance of those wiser than we are.

Right work means that the use of our energies for what is necessary and profitable. Right conditions implies School work. Salvation on Earth means, in fact, to find our own right School and to devote ourselves to it, finding in it our values and our support.

---

*Here means the pattern of our nature, our essence.

The Natural Life on earth is not sufficient. Salvation on Earth means to be protected from evil. "Lead us not into temptation, but deliver us from evil". We must learn not to trust in our own strength. Salvation on Earth is the same as *right living*.

This stage is reached gradually from the previous one. There is no sharp transition except in some mystical schools where 'mortification' is practised (cf. Gerson: *sudden* order to abandon mortification and take up active duties).

At this stage the person has already full responsibilities as a teacher. He has gained the certainty of the Way he is following and he cannot evade the duty of passing on his certainty. This does not belong to his own becoming but to love. He makes sacrifices for love alone to help others. The true School begins here, because there is a real link with higher levels of being. The teacher has a real knowledge differing from ordinary knowledge, not only by transmission from higher levels, but from his own direct experience.

The teacher and the School are one. He teaches what he knows. At this stage of the Work there is adaptation to the Laws of the Earth. The teacher knows his own limitations and the limitations of any man who is not fully grounded in eternal life. He must so order his life in time that he can find a path to eternal life.

By his own direct knowledge and experience he is delivered from doubt. He knows the taste of Salvation beyond time and space. In the Mystic Way this is the stage of *Illumination*. Nevertheless he is still unable to pass freely into higher centers and therefore he can have periods of darkness, when he seems to have lost the way and he only keeps going forward because of the general momentum of the work he has created. 'The Dark Night of the Soul', is the state of *Man No.4* when his higher experiences withdraw entirely from him and he sees himself bound under the Laws of the Earth. He realizes that he has not finally cast off the laws of the moon and that he must sacrifice entirely and forever the 'lower self' which is subject to these laws.* Hence his stage is also called *mortification*.

---

*See above, the section "Earthly Life." The note *Sol* in the octave is the stage of maximum uncertainty, a point of tension between the 'beginning' and the 'end'. Gurdjieff called it the *harnel-aoot*.

Man No.4 in religion is known as the righteous man after his conversion. The Beatitudes: Poor in Spirit - Mourn - Meek - Hunger and Thirst - Merciful - Pure in Heart - Peacemaker - Persecuted, all apply fully to Man No.4.

Nevertheless his work must continue on Earth. He must create conditions into which the typical Laws of the Earth opposed to the Work cannot penetrate. This is the 'ark-building' stage of the Work, helping to form a link between the 'inner circle' of humanity and the 'circle of confusion of tongues'.

This stage of becoming can take many forms. It all depends upon the previous stage whether it opens up the fullest possibilities. Every compromise, every missed opportunity weakens by so much the power of the next stage. Therefore an infinite gradation of states is possible. A man may reach this stage and fulfill only a part of its possibilities. But he cannot stop here because its essence is to be a transition. It is the 'middle of the way'. He must go on or go back. There is still no guarantee of salvation. His guarantee is outward rather than inward - in the conditions he has created round him. The inward decision is all important for *fa* is now reinforced by external conditions of life which characterise *sol*. The work is on Earth and belongs to the Earth. He enters higher worlds, but only as a visitor who must return to his own level.

So long as we live on the Earth and our consciousness is centered mainly in our physical bodies, in other words, so long as the center of gravity of our being is H48*, we are bound to the Laws of the Earth and we must recognize and submit to their consequences. There can be no guarantee of salvation. We can only look for probabilities and not certainties. Life in time and space is governed by laws of probability, not laws of certainty. We must try and increase the probabilities of right states and decrease the risk of bad states by the use of right methods and by seeking right conditions of work.

---

*H48 or "hydrogen 48" is the name Gurdjieff gave to the substance of man's ordinary experience - thought, feelings etc. True self-conscious experience is H24 and self-transforming power is H12. H6 is the universal substance of All Worlds. A good commentary on this scheme from the point of view of Samkhya philosophy is to be found in Lizelle Reymond's *To Live Within*, Doubleday & Co., 1971.

There is a different part of us, to which the laws of the earth do not apply. In this we find our own selves eternally.

LA. *Salvation in World 24* (The Planetary World)

In this stage we fulfill our own Destiny. This is not in time, but in eternity. We become eternally ourselves. We are liberated from accident. This is the realm of super-effort. The essence must be freed from illusions of time and space: life on Earth as necessary activity only.

Immortality begins here through the formation of what Gurdjieff called the second body: the flowering of the inward life.

True self-consciousness is obtained and awakening of the Higher Emotional Center. There is not only *being* but *doing.* We accomplish *the task* we were given to do. The Planetary World is the world of the Individual Self. In this world I seek my own perfection: everything that purifies my being and everything that liberates my will. But above all, we enter Eternity. This is not the world of Space and Time. "Everything that comes into existence carries within it the seeds of its own dissolution" (Buddha). Such is the law of Space and Time. But not the Law of Eternity.

The Planetary World is also the world of the Union of Essences. Here is true marriage, true friendship which is not subject to change.

Therefore, Salvation in the Planetary World means the eternal possession of

1. Ourselves
2. Our true relationships
3. The task we are fated to accomplish

The man who fulfills this stage is *Man No.5.*

He has secured his Eternal Salvation.
He exists beyond time and space.
He has knowledge of Immortality.
He lives in his awakened Essence.
He fulfills his own Fate.
He creates and has created his own Being - his own self.
He knows the Self above himself, but has not united with it.

This is the 'Third Awakening'. The eternal self comes to conscious birth. The essence awakens and becomes active. Permanent 'I' begins to dominate. The physical body and its senses and modes of cognition are no longer the only part which he can control. He *feels* himself in eternity. The sacrifices of the previous stage bear fruit. The dark night of the soul is seen as the dawn of the light of eternity.

The laws of fate become operative. The Teacher now embarks on his eternal destiny. He stands astride of space, time and eternity secure in the knowledge that his real self is awake and cannot die. He can now transmit, not only knowledge, but power. He has become a creator in his own right. He can overcome the Laws of the Earth.

He knows that he cannot be touched in his true self. But he also knows that he must sacrifice this self. He begins to communicate with the great Self. He knows that he belongs to himself only so that he can make the greatest sacrifice - of his real self -where previously he has only sacrificed useless imaginary things.

The true self of Man No.5 is outside the world. His School is not in time and space. He sees the eternal becoming.

There is now full unity of the Teacher - the School - and the System. All are one, because they are the expression of the eternal reality. He no longer teaches anything from second hand knowledge. Even that which is beyond and above him is known to him. All that is needed by man on Earth belongs to him in his own right.

He has everything, but at the same time he knows that he himself does not belong to himself. His eternal reality is but the reflection of the supra-eternal reality of the great Self whose expression he is 'becoming'. There is no further 'becoming in time' for him. His next step is a 'transformation in Eternity'. The line of becoming for Man No.5 has become 'invisible' on earth, no one can tell what changes occur in him, because they are non-temporal.

He is his own master and if he chooses, he can remain his own master through all eternity. He can be born where and how he wishes. *Kaivalya* in Yoga teaching is only the liberation of this self. There is the higher state of Man No.6.

SI. *The Salvation of the Sun* (the Union with Jesus)

In this stage, we *know* that the Perfected Individuality of the Sun, or Jesus, is everywhere in everything as H12 the all pervading consciousness of Individual Perfection. Jesus is in me, in the stones, in the meanest and the highest, everywhere conscious. Jesus is known as all pervading. The reality of all things is the same. We are united in Him.

'Yonder Blessed Sun. . . . . . .'

To break down the barrier which separates me from Him: "The veil of the Temple is rent".

These *words* must become living *reality*. But we cannot keep this experience unless the whole Pyramid of Salvation is built.

True salvation must mean the ever present Union with Jesus. Then all parts of our being will know Him and live by Him. But this is the state which only belongs to Man No.6. Therefore for us there can only be glimpses: but, "He that believeth on me shall not perish, but have Everlasting Life."

Once to have known and seen the Truth is a great thing, but it is not *salvation.*

According to our system there is a level of being which is symbolised as H12, which is perfect self-consciousness. This is beyond space and time and it is therefore "immanent" in all that exists. There is no place and no time that is not pervaded with H12. That means that perfect self-consciousness is everywhere.

In religious terms this means that the Divine Consciousness is everywhere. This is the State of Jesus-in Hindu teaching the *Atman* or Great Self.

The great step from Man No.5 to Man No.6 is the Union of his own self with the Great Self, the surrender of the self-created Self to Jesus. This is: Salvation beyond eternity; the transcending of personal Fate; the Life of the Sun.

Jesus gives himself to the self. The self gives itself to Jesus. Both are equal. One from above, one from below. They fit perfectly because Jesus surrenders his utter perfection to meet the limited perfection of His lover.

The created self is now safe from all harm for it has passed beyond even the becoming of eternity. But its work on earth is not complete. It must share in the work of the world.

The teacher has now become the Way. He is the incarnation of Jesus of earth. He has no separate self-hood of his own. He has abandoned not only the illusory self, but even the real self of his eternal essence. All have been sacrificed to Jesus. His will is the will of Jesus. He lives by the Universal Self of the 'Universe'.

Nevertheless he is still not one with God, for he is an individual. He can know moments of perfect transcendence when all individuality - even the perfect individuality of Jesus - is merged into the Universal Love. But he is not one with the Trinity.

The Salvation of Man No.6 is ineffable. He is beyond all categories of separate existence. There is no self in the Universe into which he does not enter. His compassion embraces all things. He has no fate. He has nothing whatever which he calls his own.

Jesus is the One Self from Above - Buddha is the One Self from Below.

DO. *The Highest State*

When a man - or rather a Being - can draw freely from the Source of all Being, the Hydrogen 6 which is beyond all individual existence, he is free for ever from danger. He is beyond time and space, beyond eternity, beyond individuation, above all worlds, all partial and incomplete forms of existence. He can be or not be whatever he wishes. The perfection of this state is Man No.7.

We must understand that the Levels of Man are not to be understood in temporal succession. This applies only to the transition to Man No.5, who finds himself in eternity *through his life in time.* The higher levels are of a different order. They do not belong to *me,* it is not *my* salvation that is at stake.

The knowledge that I am Jesus does not belong to time and space. It is not and cannot be true in time and space. Even eternal life touches only the fringe of it. The knowledge of *supra-individuation* is *beyond all experience.* It is the only *numinous* experience to which the word should apply.

Because he can enter freely into the Universal Being, all individual existence is subject to Him. He is Jesus - Buddha - the Sun and all Suns. He is God. No laws can touch him, for he goes beyond all forms of existence into the pure potency of World 6.

Whether we realize it or not, Jesus is within us. No one is less Jesus or more Jesus because of his own state, for Jesus is everything. Every stone, every blade of grass is Jesus. The perfect Consciousness participates in all experience: wherever there is the feeling of 'I'-whether this is fragmentary or united-Jesus is always there.

There is not time nor space, nor eternity, no distinction of 'this' or 'that', no separation of 'I' and 'Thou'. Therefore Jesus enters into all joy and all suffering. He partakes in all good deeds and all evil deeds. He is the Sinner of sinners and The Saint of Saints. This is the crucifixion of Jesus-that all experience must be His.

From this there is no deviation. Therefore there is no *attainment* in union with Jesus for we are united with Him beyond time and beyond eternity.

Atman is *Brahman. Tat twam asi. Sa Atman.* "The Brahman is not a Self and yet the Self is Brahman" this is the true interpretation.

The Individual is not set against the Universal. It is merely one manifestation to which we happen to belong.

So long as any individuality exists there is imperfect harmony between the part and the whole. The highest in Man is called in our system the Higher Mental Centre. This is only an expression for the supra-individual consciousness of H6.

When man has a momentary glimpse of this state, he knows a rapture beyond all description. This is possible even for Man No.4. To pass into this state and remain connected with it belongs to Man No.6. But the full liberation from the bonds of individual existence is the characteristic of Man No.7. There is no higher state possible, for this is final liberation.

Salvation is perfect when the Individual ceases to be individual in his highest level. Then the Above One - the One - and the Many are in harmony. Such a man can live on earth, but he has no ties which bind him anywhere.

The Jesus state is perfect individuality, but this is only one aspect of the true Jesus. Man No.7 has penetrated beyond to the state where no materialized being remains - only the pure potency of the Six Triads.

There is no time, no eternity, no space, no number, no distinction of 'I' and 'not-I', no limitations of being of any kind, no fate, no doing or non-doing - only fullness, the immensity of Universal Existence. Suffering all suffering, rejoicing in all Joy belongs to Jesus. Beyond this is the All which does not distinguish.

All becoming whatsoever ceases, for the Ultimate Triad is now One.

For Jesus there is a distinction between Becoming and Love. Therefore real sacrifice is possible. Jesus gains all and sacrifices all. This is shared by Man No.6.

Man No.7 corresponds to the Unknown Jesus, withdrawn into the ineffable glory of the Trinity. He works as Creator. He alone has power to change the course of Nature. Ten thousand million souls depend upon him.

Nevertheless the Historical Jesus is greater still, for he is not Man, but God.*

---

*This obscure idea is probably taken from an incident in which Gurdjieff referred to Jesus as Man No.8.

Intermediate States
of Salvation

It being obvious that the perfect salvation which belongs to Man No.7 is the rarest of events, it becomes necessary to enquire as to the intermediate levels. Does Man No.6 go so far and simply *fail* to go farther, or is his destiny fulfilled by the Union with Jesus? Is it possible to conceive Man No.5 who does not make the next great step of renunciation and who yet can be called good and great?

These questions refer to a great mystery, which cannot be solved by the category of *becoming* only. If becoming were the only criterion of value, it would be inconceivable that there should be any state at which becoming ceased. The step diagram* shows us that becoming is only one element in the Ultimate Triad. Every being has his own place in the Universal scale and this place corresponds to his being as well as to his capacity for becoming.

Though man belongs by his nature to the category of becoming, it does not follow that he must reach the highest level or fail. On the contrary, there is for each individual a destiny which represents the full realization of his possibilities.

---

*cf. P.D. Ouspensky *In Search of the Miraculous*, Routledge & Kegan Paul, 1977, pp. 322-4. The step diagram or 'the diagram of everything living' depicts the totality of beings as an organized whole. Everything has its place according to the food it eats, what it is food for and the kind of substance which, basically it *is*. In Gurdjieff's *Beelzebub's Tales to His Grandson* the idea is presented in a multitude of vivid ways, centered on the doctrine of *reciprocal maintenance*, a cosmic ecology *par excellence*.

This is of great importance for our understanding of life on Earth.

Each man and woman has his or her own fate - corresponding to essence. The realization of this fate in its full significance means the awakening of the essence. This is the level of note *la* in the Octave of Salvation. The remaining notes do not belong to time or eternity and it is impossible to understand how they are or are not achieved. This is the mystery which our minds cannot penetrate.

Not all are united with Jesus, but Jesus is united with all. There are many possibilities of union which for us are both different and not different.

But this is the fundamental principle of Salvation - that man must create his own self. The rest is beyond our ken.

What then of those who do not reach the level of Man No.5? Do they fail? This cannot be answered in time, for essence does not exist in this time alone. It is necessary to take eternal recurrence into account. But this implies that the octave must be alive. This is the only indispensable requirement.

Everyone can be saved in so far as his octave is alive; but salvation only begins when the 'interval' is passed. After that the possibilities are infinite.

The Depths of Self Realization

The Realization of Self. Man No.5 (LA)

According to our system there is a part of man which is his own eternally. The laws of the planetary world permit and require the existence of entities separated from one another in time, space and eternity and distinguishable units from other similar units. According to this doctrine the essence is something more than simple 'being.' It contains the residual possibilities of free development which the Laws of World 24 allow. In other words the essence is a real living being. It has a single infinite set of possibilities of growth and development. Our life in time is one out of this singly infinite set of possibilities. This means that we live in one less dimension than we are entitled to. The extra dimension is *eternity* which is measured by consciousness. The growth of the essence thus requires an increase of consciousness.

It must, of course, be understood that 'extension' in eternity is not spacelike. It is not an addition to the corporeal nature of man, a 'thickening' of his physical body - or even his time body - in a fifth dimension. It is a greater and fuller *existence*.

'Extension' in eternity depends upon the level of consciousness or the quality of being that a man possesses. Every increase in the true level of consciousness therefore enlarges proportionately the possibilities of the essence.

By 'true level' of consciousness is meant the quantity of consciousness permanently available as distinct from the highest point reached momentarily in the fluctuations of state.

There is a threshold at which the consciousness of the essence is sufficient to permit movement in the fifth dimension. This is the Second Awakening, when man really ceases to be a machine and gains true power of choice. This differs from the choice possible for sleeping man which is confined to a moment of time. The choice before the awakened essence is above time and therefore can produce permanent changes in time.

These considerations explain the nature of the transition from Man No.4 to Man No.5. The work of Man No.4 is directed above all to the increase of consciousness. He must struggle against and overcome all the processes in him which waste conscious energy. He must increase energy and he must increase the work of his 'chemical factory' until his consciousness begins to overflow his life in time. The crux of this work is the withdrawal of consciousness from the 'earthly selves' from the imaginary 'I' which gives a false sense of personality to the multiplicity of experience in the lower centers. This is a long and painful struggle. It means that his earthly selves - the selves which are formed under the Laws of the Earth - must die and they must die consciously. This is the meaning of the aphorism 'to wake up - to die - to be born again'. The earthly selves must die in order that the Planetary Self - the self of the Essence - should be born. This is variously described as 'crystallisation', the 'growth of the astral body', and the 'awakening of essence'. It comes from the struggle of 'yes' and 'no'. This means the rejection of all values which conflict with this central aim. For Man No.4, this is possible because he has a permanent centre of gravity and however difficult the choice may be at a given moment, he has the power to make it. The struggle of 'yes' and 'no' is more than the choice of right actions, it means the constant withdrawal of attention -that is consciousness - from every thought and feeling that arises from his earth selves.

As this work proceeds the man begins to feel his own existence in eternity. This existence is fresh and young, but also feeble and uncertain like a child. It has the same possibilities in eternity as a child born in time. This is the true meaning of the saying: "except ye become as little children. . ."The difference between the awakening essence of Man No.5 and the growing essence of a child is that one is conscious in eternity and the other in time only. This difference is infinite and wonderful, but the likeness is also wonderful. The weariness and age of the man who has passed through the depths of experience of Man No.4 is sloughed off and an unquenchable youthfulness and an abiding joy and freshness take their place. The dark night of the soul is followed by the radiance of the eternal dawning.

With the awakening of the essence and the birth of the man's true self, the laws of fate become fully operative. The Essence has infinite freedom compared with the time-life of the earth, but is confined within the planetary laws of its Being. The laws of fate affect the life of Man 1,2 and 3 in a haphazard, uncertain fashion. At one moment the events which occur are the product of mere accident, the fortuitous conjunction of earthly pro-cesses. At another moment - particularly in states of deep emo-tional significance - the essence is touched and the laws of fate come into effect. But it is generally impossible with sleeping man to separate the consequences of accident and fate. From the moment of decision the influence of fate begins to grow, but it becomes paramount only with Man No.5. In so far as his life in time is concerned, Man No.5 is above all a *builder*. He must fulfill his eternal destiny which to build between the world of space and time and the larger world of the eternal essences a bridge across which his fellow men can pass after him. This work may take the form of artistic creation, of religious or philosophical teaching. Balzac calls such men 'Specialists'. They have knowledge and power different from that of ordinary men, but they have a well-defined special destiny to fulfull. But Balzac did not understand the difference between Man No.5 and higher levels of Man - Man No.6 and No.7.

Man No.5 has reached the fullness of individual being. His essence is awake and he knows that birth and death in time are mere aspects of his being which remain untouched by the laws of Earth.

The stage now reached is the note *la* in the Octave of Salvation. It is marked by freedom from the laws of the Earth, from the laws of accident and separation, from the laws of descent and failure, from the laws of destruction and death. In the fullness of his own being Man No.5 can have all that he desires, but only within the limits of the Planetary world. He cannot 'do' in the full sense of the word, that is produce fresh causes independent of all restrictive laws. This power belongs only to Man No.7. Man No.5 is subject to the Laws of his Own Fate and he can only overcome these laws by passing on to the next stage of Salva-tion.

In all these things there are mysteries which cannot be fathomed by the human mind and heart perceiving and judging in terms of earthly values. Compared with sleeping people, Man No.5 is a great being endowed with supernatural powers. He has a permanent 'I'. He can be in the third state of consciousness. Through consciousness in his higher emotional center he can pass beyond the limitations of space and time. He can also control as he will all his lower centers. He can live outside his physical body and he has complete mastery over it.

His relations with other people are different from those of ordinary men. He can read their minds and emotions and can produce in other people higher states of consciousness and experiences impossible for them to know unaided. These powers and the knowledge which he possesses through his awakened essence in eternity enable him to teach with authority inconceivable even in Man No.4. The School of Man No.5 is not confined to space and time. Those who can enter it must leave their earthly selves behind. His teaching is incomprehensible to the earthbound. It is beyond logic and beyond language. It speaks to the essence.

This is the true characteristic of Man No.5: that he deals in essence and not in earthly shadows. He is real himself and he is concerned with realities. The self which has awakened is his own self. He is secure in a world compared with which ours is a dream state. It must, however, be understood that all Men No.5 are not identical. It is their nature to be themselves, unique and distinct in eternity as in time and space. Each Man No. 5 has different powers and a different fate.

At the same time, Man No. 5 knows that he has not reached the final stage of salvation. He knows that attainment of free individuality is not the end of human becoming. He has experienced the supreme joy of union with the Great Self beyond all separate selves, but he is not confirmed in this experience. It does not belong to him, because he belongs to himself and the Great Self cannot be shared. Man No.5 knows that if he would advance further, he must sacrifice the self he has found and created and must cease to belong to himself at all. If he is not prepared to make this sacrifice, he is free to withhold it and his destiny is not diminished or tarnished thereby. In either case he plays his part in the cosmic scheme. He is in his own essence the bridge between time and eternity and as many as can follow him share in the Salvation he has gained. But if he goes no further he remains subject to the planetary laws and his becoming does not go beyond eternity.

Union with the Great Self. Man No.6 (SI)

Man No.5 lives under the Laws of World 24. His individuality is his own and this means that it is separate and distcinct from other individualities. Although he has infinitely greater being than Man No.4, he is still subject to the limited categories of space, time, number and eternity. In fact Man No.5 is all that sleeping man imagines himself to be - a *man* in the full sense of the word. But he is not superhuman. In becoming Man No.6, the limits of human personality are left behind. This is expressed by the diagram which shows the 'density of the middle storey' of Man of different categories.

24		12		6		3
48		24		12		6
96		48		24		12

Man 1,2,3, and 4   Man No.5   Man No.6   Man No.7

This diagram represents the three levels upon which each order can live. Man 1,2,3 and even 4 lives normally in the state of isolation which is represented by H48. He can rise to the direct perception of H24 and he can fall to the level of animal life - H96. Man No.5 lives normally in the state of free consciousness and can reach true self-consciousness at will. He can also live as an ordinary Man. Man No.6 not merely has the power of self-consciousness, but actually *is* himself on its level. He can reach up to the Universal Consciousness which is unknowable for the sleeping man.

In order to understand Man No.6 it is necessary to grasp what it means to be centered in pure self-consciousness. This involves the interpretation of the true significance of Hydrogen 12. The Being of Man No.6 must be identical with the being of the Sun. It is not merely a question of passing experience, which enters the life even of Man 1,2 and 3, nor is it the 'participation', which is possible for Man No.5. It is actual identity of being. Moreover this identity cannot be partial as the identity of one piece of wood with another. Such limited or partial identity can only have meaning under the laws of the Earth. The Laws of World 12 do not provide for any partial or separate categories. This means that Man No.6, in the very center of his being, is identical with all other Men No.6 and with every being of World 12; that is, with every Sun, or more properly with the Unmanifested Sun which is the true Being of the Sun of our experience.

All beings on the level of the Sun are one and not many. At the same time, they have identity that is true individuality. This is, for us, one of the great mysteries of existence. We cannot conceive unity without the loss of identity, but this is what the system teaches us of the Being of the Sun and therefore of the Being of Man No.6.

There is a further property of H12 which must be taken into account. It belongs to a world which is beyond the categories of space and time and yet it has a limitation corresponding to the distinction between Static Recurrence (space-number) and Kinetic Recurrence (time-eternity). This means the H12 is all pervasive; it is the focussing of consciousness into the experience of individuality, but this focussing is everywhere, always and eternal. There is no place in the universe where H12 is absent. It is the core of all experience, the Life of all selves.

In this last phrase lies the secret of Man No.6, whose very being is H12. In the Indian religions, the Self of selves is called the Atman. In Islam it is Allah. In the Hebrew Scriptures, it is Elohim, the One-Many of Creation. In Christianity it is Jesus. Jesus is the Unmanifested Sun, the pure Individuality that fills the whole Universe. *In principio erat verba* (In the beginning was the word). The terrible weakness of human language is laid bare in these words, so great in their true significance, so misleading in their temporal form. The Word, the 'I am' of God, is not in time. It has neither beginning nor end either in time or in eternity.

It is the weakness of human language that compels recourse to symbolism. The Hydrogen Table is proof against verbal misconception, but its content depends upon our own understanding. The Jesus of our System is immeasurably more real than the Jesus of the Christian religion - even more real than the Jesus of mystical experience: but His reality is transcendent. Nothing that can be ascribed to a Personal God can approach the pure individuality of H12. He is beyond our experience, unknowable and inaccessible to our minds and even to our emotion. This is the crucial fact for which religion must account. It is a problem common to all religions and a stumbling block for every creed which asserts a Personal Deity. Why can we not think God nor reach Him with our emotions if He is a Person with attributes of personality such as we can conceive? The Christian religion invokes the Trinity and declares that the Father is known by the Son, but this is an inadequate and faulty application of the Triadic principle.

The true situation is that although Jesus is conscious not only of human, but of all experience, the inverse in not possible. No being who is confined to the laws of the Earth can know Jesus. A man must first become *himself* and only then can he go beyond himself. Until his essence is awakened and he has attained unity in himself, his experiences of the higher emotional center, if they occur, are tainted with the subjectivity of earthly life. As St. John of the Cross and many another mystical teacher has emphasized, the visions and ecstatic experiences of the unpurified soul are deceptive and dangerous. Even if such a man thinks he has a 'vision' or 'audition' of Jesus, it is only imagination of the Higher Emotional Center and he is not saved thereby.

The whole scheme of Salvation for man turns on the *progressive* liberation from restrictive laws. As the Hebrew religion teaches, no man can look upon the face of God and live. This is the secret of Man No.6. He has not only looked upon the face of God, but he has become united in his very essence to the Divine Self. His own self, eternal and indestructible, is seen by him as incomplete. It is 'like the angels', perfect but limited. If he is to gain the Salvation which only Perfect Being can know, he must sacrifice his own individual identity, his own separate will. By this act he gains a fresh degree of freedom. He is no longer bound by the Laws of his own Fate. He is free from Planetary influences. No one on a lower level can tell the nature of the change, for we can only know men of higher being through their works in time and space. Any description of Man No.6 must be relative to our own experience. On our level it is possible to have moments of experience of the Higher Emotional Center. Man No.5 can pass freely between his lower centers and his Higher Emotional Center. Man No.6 has his being entirely transformed from the physical body and its centre to the Higher Emotional Center and he can enter and dwell in the Higher Mental Center.

This means that he can have the knowledge of immediate union. For him the distinction of 'I' and 'Not-I' is no barrier to experience, he enters into all the experience of all that exists. This is indicated in the diagram for H6 is the Objective Consciousness which is beyond individuality and this represents the 'higher normal' experience of Man No.6, just as H24, 'separate individuality' is his 'lower normal' state.

These indications cannot convey the miracle of Union. Not only does Man No.6 surrender himself to Jesus - Jesus also surrenders himself in the same Union. Jesus, who is never absent from man - for He is in all experience, great or lowly - unites fully and for ever with the man who surrenders all his own existence. Not even the language of the most exalted mysticism can convey the nature of this Union. It is beyond all the categories of our experience.

The doctrine of Salvation is widened and enriched by the conception of Man No.6. Man No.5 gathers together his power in his own self-created individuality. But Man No.6 leaves himself to become all. His teaching is beyond self. His school is the school of love. He can say with Jesus, "I am the Way, the Truth and the Life". His own will no longer exists and his life in time is utterly free from motives of self. He enters into the sorrows and joys of all men and through him a whole epoch is delivered from destruction. For it is only by the existence of Men No.6 in the world that a force is set against the influence of the Moon which makes salvation possible.

The salvation of Man No.6 is ineffable. It is beyond all categories of separate existence. There is no self in the Universe whose experience he does not share. His compassion embraces all beings impartially. He has no fate - nothing whatever that he can call his own.

Nevertheless this is still not the ultimate state of Salvation. Man No.6 is still an individual. He is United with Jesus and in his higher state, he reaches up to Universal Existence, but he is not confirmed there. He is within the laws of the Solar System; that is, the laws of perfect individuality. He has not the complete freedom of the pure triad. He cannot create causes. There is one more stage before the octave is complete.

The Final Realization   Man No. 7   (DO)

The abandonment of all individuality. The Self of all Selves as a mere aspect of Universal Being. The liberation of consciousness from all forms of being. The union of self with no-self. The disappearance of all distinction between self and not-self. Salvation as the pyramid of perfection. All levels of being united by the streams of upward and downward consciousness. The union of the triad of Being - Becoming - Love. The transcending of all becoming. The perfect Love which embraces all existence. Salvation as the perfection of all triads.

According to the principle of the octave, the first do already prefigures in itself the second: the final fulfillment is like an 'overtone' of the first step. The moment of beginning is unique and ineffable. This character of beginning enters into all the succeeding 'notes' or stages and it is this that enables them to develop in their own right. The second do is entirely different. In the state of final realization the sense of a movement towards that state is annihilated. The final state is totally self-sufficient. That is why in every octave the second do acts as its *Absolute*. In the octave of Salvation, the second do is God Himself. This does not mean the total reality of the whole universe, of the galaxies beyond ours and so on. It is the Free Source which is the ultimate in liberation for beings of this solar system of ours. To the question: "how then can the final liberation even have relevance to partially liberated beings?" the answer is that the octave is not only ascending but also descending. There is a movement from Above to the Below that Western man sees in the shining image of the descent of the Son of God, the Christ, from His Father upon the Earth.

We have touched upon questions of School, Teacher and Teaching. We should also bear in mind the possibilities that this very Earth is sustained and even restored and healed by the action of special men.

The state of final liberation is the Source as Father, Allah, Shiva.

The Prayer of Salvation

O Eternal Essence, O Holy Jesus, O Transcendent Godhead, grant me the keys of salvation to fulfill the destiny for which I was created, to be ready in all things to sacrifice the less for the greater and to withold nothing from the demands of Love.

Completed at Langdale   17 August 1944

TABLE OF THE OCTAVE OF SALVATION

OCTAVE	CATEGORY OF MAN	WORLD	CHARACTERISTICS
Stage or 'Note'	Gurdjieffian, Religious, Hindu and Buddhist terms	No. of Laws and Aspect of Solar System	Mystical, yogic and fourth-way terminology
DO	Man No:s 1, 2, 3	-	*Conversion* - 'the call' Magnetic center forms. The *first* Awakening.
RE	Man No:s 1,2,3	-	*Striving* - 'struggle' Formation of attitude. Learning. Conviction of *sin*.
MI	Man No:s 1,2,3	-	*Purgation* - 'emptiness' Recognizing difficulties. Realization of *nothingness*. The *second* Awakening.
INTERVAL			Help and Decision.

'Shock' →

Preparation

FA	96 Moon	Man No:s 1,2,3 *Righteous Man* *Sotapanna*	*Salvation from Moon* - 'light', 'dryness', Renunciation of negativity. Acceptance of the Way. "He who has entered the stream"
SOL	48 Earth	Man No.4 *Converted Man* *Upa Guru* *Sakadagamin*	*Salvation on Earth* - 'illumination', 'mortification', To live rightly on Earth Service "He who will return once only"
LA	24 Planets	Man No.5 *Saint* *Sadhaka Guru (Avatar)* *Anagamin*	*Salvation of Essence* - 'Kaivalya' Realization of Self. Liberation. Movement out of time. The *third* Awakening. "He who will never return"
SI	12 Sun	Man No.6 *Son of God* *Sad Guru (Mahavatar)* *Arahat*	*Salvation in Sun* - 'Atman' Union with Jesus (Great Self) Perfect Individuality. "The worthy one"
DO	6 Unmanifest Sun	Man No.7 *Reality of God* *Param Guru*	*Ultimate Realization* - 'Atman is Brahman' Final liberation. Penetration beyond the veil of existence.

Fulfillment

BOOKS:
pp. 15 16 27 52 58 67 69 94 100   106 138 153 168 169
                                    116
p16-17-18 ×35 VERY IMPORTANT : COPY FOR A.M.
                        BENNETT'S 6 DIMENSIONS
p15   18 DEFIN. OF "ACTIVE MENTATION"!

19 PSYCHIC PHENOMENA   1.
22 "LAST WORDS OF LAST BOOK......   2.
    POSSIBLE TO LIVE IN THREE WORLDS"   3.
24 STOP EXERCISE ?   4. TIME
42 "TWO PRINCIPLES OF LIVING"   5. ? HYPARXIS ? (DEFIN.) "ABLENESS
33 "PATTERN"   (P. 120) TO BE"
                                    6.
45 EXERCISE ? ZIKR ?
    PATTERN - TIME - EXPECTATIONS

46 THIS APPEARS IN THE GOSPELS
51 & 52 ZIKR - NO INSTR. 102
53 'NAMAZ'- TO DO TO GIVE BACK.
    I WANT TO DO IT - NO INSTR.
65 'MESOTERIC' (DEFIN) STAGE OF THE WORK
66 'MAGNETIC CENTER' DEFIN, & ESSENCE
                    & PERSONALITY WORK
107 TIME AS A CONDITION OF EXISTENCE (IN THIS WORLD)
114 WOW! ME TOO!
127 "5th Descent"
    & "THE KIND OF FUTURE WHERE THINGS CAN GO RIGHT WITHOUT EFFORT
        IS CLOSED IF YOU IMPOSE A PLAN." !!! JEN, SCHUFER

130 "FREED THEMSELVES FROM THE DESIRE FOR POWER"
    "ALL THE THOUGHTS WE HAD WERE REALLY FANTASIES, UNLESS THERE WAS A COMMITMENT
        TO MAKE THEM INTO SOME SORT OF REALITY."
132 ALEXANDER METHOD
133 FANTASY & DAYDREAMS = HELPLESSNESS
139 JOB (BIBLE)
67, TOP, "ESSENCE DOES NOT REASON."
101 "... NO WISH TO DO WHAT WE CAN DO." ...???
111 ORDERING ONES LIFE WITH THOUGHTFORMS
118 PREPARING FOR FUTURE THINGS ONE DOES NOT KNOW
        WILL OCCUR
122 'MENTAL IMAGES' AND PLANNING - A.M.
150 DEFINITIONS OF 3 IDIOTS!
151 "   "   " SCIENCE OF IDIOTISM
    " " MECHANICAL SAMENESS REALLY IS AN ABSENCE OF IDENTITY
25 - DESIRABLE OUTCOME ?

COPY, A.M.- 127